BEEBE & CLEGG
Their Enduring Photographic Legacy

BEEBE & CLEGG
Their Enduring Photographic Legacy

John Gruber and John Ryan assisted by Mel Patrick

Featuring 222 photographs from the Lucius M. Beebe and Charles M. Clegg Jr. Collection of the California State Railroad Museum Library & Archives

Center for Railroad Photography & Art
Madison, Wisconsin
www.railphoto-art.org

Cover: Lucius Beebe's creative view here contradicts the conventional wisdom that he only made wedge-of-pie photographs. Just at sunset, a Union Pacific train climbs the Sherman Hill grade in Wyoming. Here is a classic example of how Beebe mixed up information. His photo was used in *The Age of Steam* (1957, page 196, described as a freight train headed for Laramie, with image reversed) and as the endpaper for *Great Railroad Photographs U.S.A.* (1964, a passenger train for Cheyenne). A retired UP engineer, John Boehner, identified the location: "This is a westbound freight with a 3800 Challenger on the point. The train is just west of Otto (Mile Post 524.03) operating on Track no. 1. The engine is approaching the right-hand curve just west of MP 525.0. Note the engine is working steam, the injector is on, and there is exhaust from the pops, generator, and stoker. Probably not going very fast, about 15 to 20 mph. (Borie is MP 519.)" California State Railroad Museum, BC0835

Cover design by Phil Hamilton

Lucius Beebe (left) and Charles Clegg pose along the tracks of the Southern Pacific narrow gauge in the Owens Valley of California. Beebe's 4" by 5" Graflex Model B with an adapter for a film pack is on the ground next to him; Clegg holds his original Kodak Medalist with a black lens barrel. Clegg made the photo using a self-timer and tripod. It is on the dust jacket of *Mixed Train Daily*. California State Railroad Museum, BC3411

Book design and composition by John Gruber and John Ryan with assistance from Mel Patrick, Phil Hamilton, and Scott Lothes

Photographs copyright © 2018 California State Railroad Museum or as noted

Text copyright © 2018 John Gruber and John Ryan

All rights reserved. No part of this publication may be reproduced or transmitted in any form or by any means, electronic or mechanical, including photocopy, recording, or any other information storage and retrieval system, without prior permission from the publisher.

First published in the United States of America in 2018 by the
Center for Railroad Photography & Art
313 Price Place, Suite 13
Madison, Wisconsin 53705
www.railphoto-art.org

Copies for sale by U.S. mail or online at
www.railphoto-art.org/store/

ISBN 978-0-692-07999-7

Printed and bound in the United States of America

Facing page: Beebe and Clegg's admiration for steam, smoke, and narrow gauge are illustrated in this closeup view of Denver & Rio Grande Western no. 473. California State Railroad Museum, BC1105

Below: A quote from Lucius Beebe, typed by Charles Clegg. Peter Holloway collection

"The disfavor of envious inferiority is a boutonniere that can be worn by a gentleman all day without fading. - Lucius Beebe

Contents

Introduction, 8

1. Their Life and Times Together, 10
   Their Cameras, 32
2. Beebe and the Beginnings, 36
3. The Visual Influences, 46
4. Main Lines and Limiteds, 54
5. Short Lines: "Not as Long but Just as Wide," 98
6. On the Narrow Gauge, 152
7. Nevada and the Virginia & Truckee, 192
8. From Coast to Coast, 204
9. Their Photographic Legacy, 212
   Beebeography, 216
   Index, 218
   Acknowledgments, 224

Charles Clegg (right) and his sister, Ann Clegg Holloway, enjoy the Maryland & Pennsylvania train featured in *Life* magazine in 1947 while a guest wipes cinders from her eyes. The party celebrated the publication of *Mixed Train Daily*. Holloway collection

Introduction

By Ann Clegg Holloway

It was great fun traveling with Chuck and Lucius. I was at the wonderful party they threw for the release of *Mixed Train Daily* in 1947 on the Maryland & Pennsylvania Railroad. Very appropriately, the M&P was a short line they had photographed for the book. I treasure the copy Lucius autographed, writing: "For Chuck, who had the idea, did the work, and made the book, in gratitude and affection."

When I turned 21, Chuck invited me for my first trip west of the Potomac River. I remember flying to Denver to meet them on their private car, the *Gold Coast,* in 1949 for a twenty-first birthday celebration tour of the American West. Chuck treated me to his favorite Colorado haunts, including Denver's Brown Palace Hotel, the Stratler Arms Hotel in Colorado Springs, and the Central City Opera. We traveled to the opera in a limousine, dressed formally for the grand occasion.

From Denver we made stops at Pueblo, Salida, and other locations, until we arrived in Carson City on the Virginia & Truckee, where they kept the car under a cottonwood tree. Traveling on the *Gold Coast* with Chuck provided a variety of experiences. We would go from sitting in the formal dining room in elegant dress for dinner to rushing to the observation platform as the train slowed down, passing by small stations, to toss coins to small children—a rail travel tradition.

But there also was a serious, lesser known reason for these trips. Chuck and Lucius continually promoted their books, and at stops they invited editors and reporters aboard the car to learn about their latest project. In a few days, a story usually appeared in the newspapers and sometimes a local magazine as well.

They introduced me to Virginia City, where my son, Peter, later designed a house for us built on the foundations of their swimming pool. My family owns the house today.

There were other trips as well. My husband, Jack, and I joined Chuck and Lucius on their second car, the *Virginia City*, in Albany, New York, in the middle of January when we were living in Utica, New York. We took our two little boys with us. We had a lovely cocktail hour and afterwards we had an elegant dinner served by their steward. By the time we finished dessert and had some dessert wine, we were dropped off in Utica in the middle of the night. It was 1:30 or 2 o'clock in the morning. The train stopped just for us to get off. We were on the platform with these two sleepy little boys, freezing, bitter cold. Not a soul in sight. No moon, no lights whatsoever. My husband turned to me and said, "well, I guess it was worth it." So we had a wonderful time.

Chuck, my older brother, looked after me and made sure I was a part of the activities. I always will be grateful for that. He loved railroads, he loved making pictures of them, and he passed his enthusiasms along to me, so it was with pleasure that I placed the Beebe/Clegg collection at the California State Railroad Museum library in Sacramento.

This book brings back wonderful memories for me, and I hope you, the reader, also will enjoy the work of my brother Chuck and of Lucius Beebe.

Virginia City, Nevada, September 2016

1 Their Life and Times Together

By using dramatic images and sweeping promotional strategies towards the end of the Depression in the late 1930s, Lucius Beebe—joined in 1941 by his life partner Charles Clegg—introduced railroad photography and the world of railroading to wide popular audiences. Their pioneering efforts established a broad market and wide appreciation for rail photography, leading to its far-reaching appeal today in print and on the internet, especially in social media where a younger audience now devours railroad images.

Friends of Beebe and Clegg say that unlike the public image Beebe crafted of themselves as sophisticated New Yorkers, they were down-to-earth "nice guys," friendly and hard working—people who knew everybody. These characteristics contrast sharply with their reputation for flamboyance, which they demonstrated vividly in both their published prose and their splashy lifestyle. It was, in part, an act—but also fun, and therefore real.

There is no denying Beebe's celebrity status. He achieved it well before Clegg came on the scene, and it helped him get a start in the book business. Beebe considered himself a Renaissance Man, a knowledgeable person dedicated to excellence. In an autobiographical note he sent in 1966 to Herb Caen, a columnist for the *San Francisco Chronicle,* he named twenty-one people he considered Renaissance Men and Women, who had "a knowledge and appreciation of excellence." Most were associates from New York and Washington, D.C., but he included on his list the architect Frank Lloyd Wright, whom he had never met. "They wrote, edited, acted, whored, drank, sang songs, served the nation, wrote history, and made enemies in their own pattern," Beebe wrote to Caen.[1]

It is difficult to establish how Beebe became so fascinated with railroads and photography. In the 1930s, he started writing about his railroad interests in books and newspapers and assumed a leading role in rail festivals in Cleveland and St. Louis. Then in 1938, he ventured into photography books. Before Beebe began creating them, about the only railroad photography book in existence had been written for children by Robert Selph Henry (1889–1970), a public relations executive for the Association of American Railroads.[2]

Beebe and Clegg met for the first time in April 1941 at a brunch in Washington, D.C., hosted by Evalyn Walsh McLean, owner of the Hope Diamond, at her estate Friendship. Beebe was visiting from New York City. Clegg, who lived in Washington, had come to the party with J. Edgar Hoover, director of the Federal Bureau of Investigation.[3]

At the end of the brunch, Mrs. McLean invited Beebe and Clegg to join her in the bar "to dish the dirt," Clegg recalled. They were house guests at Friendship and shared a connecting bathroom. Clegg left for a night on the town with friends. When he returned, he found Beebe asleep "in some disarray" in the bathtub. He woke him, cleaned up some spots of blood, and helped him to bed, Clegg wrote in the introduction to *The Lucius Beebe Reader.*[4] Clegg said their "mutual bad behavior enchanted each other."[5]

Jerome Zerbe, a guest and photographer at the 1941 brunch, confirms in his albums that Hoover and Beebe were there. A week later, another Zerbe

Clegg and Beebe strike a serious pose to show off their newspaper, the *Territorial Enterprise,* in the office in their home, the John Piper House, in Virginia City, Nevada. California State Railroad Museum, BCP0619

Clegg poses with his sister, Ann, at their homes in Rhode Island (left, 1939) and Ohio (bottom) and with the family dogs in Ohio (below). Holloway collection

photo shows Beebe and Clegg together.

Clegg soon moved from Washington, D.C., to Beebe's suite at the Madison Hotel in New York City. They were together for the rest of Beebe's life. Clegg's term of endearment for Beebe, recorded in Clegg's day-to-day calendars, was Lukey. During this time and within certain elements of the upper classes of New York City society, openly gay men and women were accepted, even as couples. Beebe and Clegg likely experienced that same acceptance. The same was true in Los Angeles and in Washington. The same was not true outside these circles, where stark discrimination existed against same-sex relations at any level.

For the next quarter of a century, they compiled an impressive publishing record, while Beebe also provided a prolific outpouring of texts for newspaper columns and national magazines such as *Holiday, Town & Country, Esquire, Ford Times, Gourmet,* and *This Week.* Some prefer to remember Beebe in a negative way for his distortions, such as when he misrepresented an illustration of the Northern Pacific from *Harper's Weekly* as a construction scene on the Denver & Rio Grande in Colorado.[6] Regardless, he remains a giant in the field of railroad journalism.

Beebe was the public face of the pair, especially in correspondence, but they worked as a team. While Beebe was a florid writer, Clegg had better organization and was fussy about spelling. With Beebe's permission, Clegg edited some of Beebe's long and difficult texts, according to Clegg's sister, Ann Clegg Holloway.[7]

Beebe (1902–1966) was older, with an established record of accomplishments in publications by the time he met Clegg. He wrote about Café Society in a syndicated column, "This New York," for the *New York Herald Tribune,* beginning in 1934, a considerable literary achievement. On the photographic side, he likely learned about photographic technique from Jerome Zerbe (1904–1988), a Café Society photographer who had been Beebe's companion in the 1930s. Beebe also may have learned

Guests at Evalyn Walsh McLean's spring brunch in 1941 included Paulette Guffey and J. Edgar Hoover (top) and Ann Carol Meem; Hal Phyfe, photographer of Manhattan high society; Lucius Beebe; and Ned McLean, son of Evalyn, married to Miss Meem (above). Photos by Jerome Zerbe, Jerome Zerbe Photographs and Papers. General Collection, Beinecke Rare Book and Manuscript Library, © 2018, Yale University

Clegg and Beebe, about a week after they met. Photo by Jerome Zerbe, Jerome Zerbe Photographs and Papers. General Collection, Beinecke Rare Book and Manuscript Library, © 2018, Yale University

about photography from the staff photographers at the *Herald Tribune*.

Charles Myron Clegg Jr. (1916–1979) was born in Youngstown, Ohio, to Ruth Standish Clegg (1897–1972) and Charles M. Clegg Sr. (1893–1970). He was a licensed ham radio operator by the time he was twelve. He had a natural interest in electronics, technology, and communications. He once wired his parents' bed with an electrical coil and bugged the living room so he could listen to party conversation from his bedroom. After his parents divorced, he and his siblings moved with their mother to Rhode Island where they lived with her father, Granville Searcy Standish. Clegg graduated from Hope High School in Providence. On his twenty-first birthday, his grandfather gave Clegg a note saying he had done everything he could for him and now that he was twenty-one, he should be out of the house by sundown.[8] Clegg moved in with his father in Washington, D.C. He took a job at Garfinckel's Department Store, a high-end emporium where Clegg met the upper crust of Washington society. Later, in New York, he was a floorwalker (floor manager) for Arnold Constable & Company, a small and fashionable department store.

When he learned of the attack on Pearl Harbor on December 7, 1941, Clegg volunteered the next day for the Navy Reserve. He was accepted immediately but was not called to report for active duty until March 2, 1942. He was sent home in an ill-fitting standard-issue uniform but quickly had a more satisfactory version sewn by a New York tailor.

Clegg's departure merited a short note in Zerbe's diary on April 23. "Lucius is in mourning. Upset as Chuck Clegg has been sent to saddle school in Kansas," wrote Zerbe, who had first mentioned Clegg in his diary earlier in 1942.[9] Clegg reported not to Kansas but to Stillwater, Oklahoma, for training as a radio technician. He then transferred to Washington, D.C., and Treasure Island, San Francisco. At each location there were almost nightly farewell parties. Although he hated air travel, Beebe flew to San Francisco to spend weekends with Clegg. In *Snoot If You Must* (dedicated to Clegg "to make him laugh"), Beebe's account of their travels ends in San Francisco.[10] Clegg was shipped to the South Pacific on the *U.S.S. Patuxent,* sailing from San Francisco on April 29, 1943.[11]

Clegg was not immune to discrimination against gays and received a dishonorable discharge on January 5, 1944. At the time, he was stationed at a naval base in Noumea, New Caledonia; details are in memos of November 3 and December 20, 1943, not included in his service record at the National Personnel Records Center in St. Louis.[12]

Upon returning to New York, Clegg launched a luxury information service called Gotham DeLuxe.[13] Beebe and Mrs. Clara Bell Walsh, a New York society hostess, were silent partners, but Clegg closed it for a lack of "legitimate-minded customers."[14]

Beebe's reputation continued to attract attention in articles and books. For example, partly in jest, Bennett Cerf wrote of Beebe's column about "the foibles in the idle rich," saying: "When he wasn't concocting drivel for his "This New York" column in the Saturday *Herald Tribune,* Beebe turned out several absolutely first-rate books on American railroading."[15] *Carolina Blues* (1944), featuring an all African-American cast, has a ten-minute dance named for Beebe. In a recruiting program he narrated for the U.S. Army about building the transcontinental railroad and the golden spike ceremony in 1869, Beebe was called the "foremost authority" on the history of American railroads.[16]

Always happy to put his name in front of the public, Beebe used his celebrity status to endorse

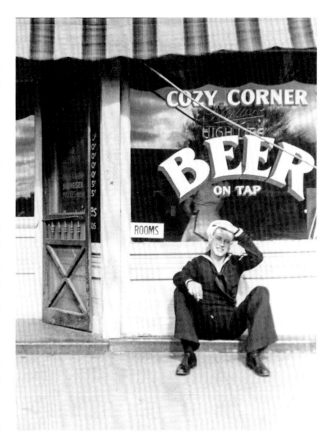

Clegg was stationed in Stillwater, Oklahoma, from May to July 1942 for training as a radio technician. Snapshots show the fun-filed times when he was off duty: sitting in front of a bar, riding a horse pulling the beer wagon, and staging a fake arrest with an officer. Holloway collection

In San Francisco, Beebe and Clegg stayed at the Palace Hotel, Beebe's favorite spot. Clegg relaxes with a large bottle (above). The partners are at dinner (top). Clegg was stationed at Treasure Island from August to December 1942 to finish training as a radio/radar technician. Holloway collection products for advertisers such as Old Angus Scotch, Aqua Velva, Calobar Sunglasses, and Studebaker automobiles. Ads for Graflex contained his advice for amateurs, saying: "Although he warns that most railroad fans are 'crazy as bedbugs,' Beebe is anxious to give advice to prospective train photographers: 'In photographing steam engines,' he says, 'smoke— as an index of action is an absolute requisite!'"[17]

Once in New York, Clegg developed a deep interest in railroading. To pursue his photography, he purchased darkroom equipment and a Medalist camera, and hired J. Ghislain Lootens (1901–1946) to give him a crash course in photography. Lootens, who taught classes at the Brooklyn YMCA, was among the prominent pictorial photographers. *Lootens on Photographic Enlarging and Print Quality* (1944) showcased his pictorial style. Clegg attributed his sense of framing a shot to Lootens, who recommended placing an object in the foreground to give depth to the picture. (See herein "Their Cameras," page 33, by Mel Patrick.)

Clegg's distinctive perspective quickly surfaced in *Trains in Transition*, released in late 1945, his first book with Beebe, which contained sixty Clegg photographs.

In 1946 the two set off on a nationwide tour to document the vanishing railroad short lines and steam locomotives in rural America, using a list of lines that had existed in 1940 as a starting point.[19] This became *Mixed Train Daily*, their most renowned work. (See Chapter 5.)

Beebe charmed railroad managements into granting them unlimited access, which resulted in photographic opportunities such as the 1946 trip in narrow gauge business cars on the soon-to-be-abandoned Rio Grande Southern in southwestern Colorado. Alfred E. Perlman, the Denver & Rio Grande Western's chief engineer (later, executive vice president of the Rio Grande and president of the New York Central and Western Pacific), served as host and became a lifelong friend. A newspaper reporter helped arrange the RGS trip and wrote a daily column about it. Then, as always, Beebe and

Clegg (top) poses in a studio portrait in 1942 with his tattoo, added while he was in the Navy. Beebe has an identical tattoo (above). Holloway collection

Beebe stands trackside somewhere in the west with his Speed Graphic nearby on the ballast. It is the "wartime" version with the black lens board instead of chrome. Holloway collection

such as Joseph Costa, a prominent New York newspaper photographer.

Mixed Train Daily: A Book of Short-Line Railroads, released in 1947, represented a maturation of the authors' work, coupling good research and photography with skilled promotion epitomized by national coverage such as "*Life* Goes to a Party" in the country's leading pictorial weekly.[21]

Clegg's sister, Ann Clegg Holloway, then a student at George Washington University, described the experience. "It was a great party. It was drinks and drinks and drinks. The band played music and people danced as we were going along. It went very slowly down through Maryland and into Pennsylvania. It was a real mixed train, it had passengers, cargo, and mail." The host was the Maryland & Pennsylvania railroad, which was among those covered in the book.

"My brother was wonderful to me," his sister said. "My mother and father got a divorce when I was 6. Chuck took over as a father image to me. And all my life he was great to me, to my family, to my kids—all of us. I was the sole survivor in his trust. Luckily, it was wonderful. When he was living here [in Virginia City], Chuck had Charlie and Peter, the middle two of four children (Jay, Charlie, Peter, Sally) come and do work for him. They worked on the Beebe House, and anything else that needed doing. Then he wined and dined them. He was good to my kids, good to me, got along great with my husband."[22]

Clegg took advantage of every opportunity to put themselves in the press.[20]

Their skills at building professional friendships, known today as networking, also extended to railroad suppliers. Beebe, aided by Willard Morgan, publisher and editor of *Camera Encyclopedia,* C. B. Peck, editor of *Railway Mechanical Engineer,* and Patrick O'Sheel, transportation editor of *Life,* selected fifty-three photos for American Locomotive Company's 1947 calendar. Beebe supported Alco's goal, recorded in the calendar introduction, "to encourage amateurs and professionals everywhere to make significant contributions to the history of railroading." The same year, he and Clegg judged a Lionel model train contest with others

In March 1948 Beebe and Clegg purchased a wooden private railroad car from the Georgia Northern.[23] They wanted their St. Bernard dog, Mr. T-Bone Towser, to be able to travel with them. They named the car the *Gold Coast* and wrote three books while living aboard it during the summers of 1948 to 1950 under a cottonwood tree in the Virginia & Truckee railroad yards in Carson City, Nevada. Alma Dettinger of WQRX New York recorded an interview with them about one of the books, *U.S. West: The Saga of Wells Fargo.*[24]

Beebe did everything he could to save the V&T

Clegg and Beebe with illustrator E. S. Hammack (center) at a book signing for *Legends of the Comstock Lode* (1950) in Virginia City, Nevada. California State Railroad Museum BCP1120

from abandonment. He tried to persuade the *Herald Tribune* owners (descendants of Darius Ogden Mills, a builder of the railroad) not to dismantle the V&T. Beebe and Clegg hurriedly wrote *Virginia & Truckee: A Story of Virginia City and Comstock Times* (1949) as part of a campaign to keep the line running. Their lack of success was one of Beebe's biggest disappointments and the eighty-year old short line ceased operation on May 30, 1950.

Before the abandonment, they moved the *Gold Coast* to Southern Pacific tracks at Sparks, Nevada. Because railroads became increasingly reluctant to handle wood cars, Beebe and Clegg purchased an all-steel, 1928 air-conditioned Pullman car named *Golden Peak* in 1954. They had it completely redone by Hollywood interior designer Robert T. Hanley, who also had decorated the *Gold Coast* and their two houses. The *Golden Peak* was rechristened the *Virginia City*. After a brief period of owning two private cars simultaneously, Beebe and Clegg presented the *Gold Coast* to the Pacific Coast Chapter of the Railway & Locomotive Historical Society in November 1954. It is on display at the California State Railroad Museum in Sacramento. The *Virginia City,* their second car, still plies the rails under private ownership and operates in charter service.

To staff their cars they hired waiters and chefs from the Southern Pacific dining car pool. Their

Beebe and Clegg enjoying being photographed with friends, often holding glasses of champagne. The top photo, in 1944, shows Ray (no last name) in the center. People in the bottom photo are not identified. Holloway collection

chef, Hazzie Wallace (1893–1972), Los Angeles, worked for the SP for more than twenty years. After retirement, he and his wife, Irene, were popular volunteers at the South Park Recreation Center, where his many activities included cooking.

While Beebe and Clegg lived aboard their railroad car in Nevada, they maintained their official residence at the Madison Hotel in New York City, traveling back and forth as required. The two ultimately decided to move west; Beebe purchased their home in Virginia City in the summer of 1949.

It was no April Fool's Day joke on April 1, 1950, when Beebe resigned from the *Herald Tribune* after twenty-one years. His column had been discontinued in 1944, but he continued to write for the editorial and drama pages. When accepting his letter of resignation, Managing Editor George A. Cornish wrote, "While your early morning and late evening hours almost never met up with my day and evening schedule it was always good to think of you in your familiar spot in the drama department. I shall like to feel that we have merely lent you to the Far West."[25]

In his farewell to New York, "I Saw the Elephant" in *Holiday*, Beebe himself wrote, "I am taking it on the lam for the same reason the wise guest goes before the party is over. The last part of every party is *not* the best, and the discerning person leaves before the band gets tired and he himself starts walking with legs akimbo."[26]

Beebe and Clegg's home in Virginia City had been owned by Dan Connors, who had come to Nevada in 1897 to cover the Corbett-Fitzsimmons fight. The Piper family, owners of Piper's Opera House, at one time also owned the home. Beebe was proud of its association with the theater. "Taking ownership required extracting an itinerant cowboy (later expanded by Beebe to two cowboys and their horses) from the front parlor," a Virginia City resident, Andria Daley, wrote in "Boardwalk Bons Vivants."[27]

In 1950, Clegg, while staying at the Bonanza Inn (the old Wells Fargo mansion), set about restoring their house, adding elaborate gardens, a swimming pool, six-car garage for Beebe's Rolls-Royces and Clegg's Jaguar, an internal fire-suppression system with a 2,000 gallon tank, and a fireproof, walk-in vault to protect their manuscripts and papers. They drove cars from the east and established residency in time to send their first Christmas cards from their new home, which they called the John Piper House.

"They became Nevadans to the core and their adventures brightened the Northern Nevada horizon for a score of years," a Reno columnist recalled.[28] Beebe staged an annual production in the state capitol, with parts portrayed by state officials including then-Governor Charles Russell.

In 1952, they purchased the *Virginia City News*, with rights to the name of the historic newspaper, the *Territorial Enterprise*. Their first edition appeared on May 2, 1952, as Volume 98, Number 18. They flipped a coin. Clegg became editor, Beebe publisher. Their joint statement said: "We propose without contrived archaism to recreate something of the identity and personality this newspaper achieved in the great days of the Comstock and to this end are reverting to its original style and title as the *Territorial Enterprise*."

Books continued. Together they produced *Hear the Train Blow* and *The American West*. Beebe alone was responsible for *Comstock Commotion*.

They went on the (rail)road to promote the books, the newspaper, and Virginia City. Each spring they would return for another adventure. In 1956 they took a six-week, 10,000-mile tour with the *Virginia City,* ending in Portland, Oregon. The *Enterprise* reported: "Front page newspaper publicity throughout the nation such as Virginia City has not known since the days of the bonanzas, magazine space values in scores of thousands of dollars and radio audiences estimated in tens of millions have been achieved for the Comstock."[29] The uncredited article had all the earmarks of Beebe's prose. The *New York Times* joined the parade of papers covering the trip.[30]

Clarence Watkins serves dinner in Beebe and Clegg's railroad car, *Virginia City*. The chef, Hazzie Wallace, is unseen, back in the kitchen. On other occasions Charlie Yee and Willie Brown served as chefs. The partners hired staff from the Southern Pacific dining car department for their car. This photo appeared in many publications including the *Illustrated London News* (January 28, 1956). After seeing this photo, Queen Juliana of Holland tried to buy the car. California State Railroad Museum, BCP0859

Beebe and Clegg show off their newspaper, the *Territorial Enterprise,* to Byron Harvey (left) and James Hart aboard the *Virginia City* in Chicago. Byron's father founded the Fred Harvey companies which operated restaurants, hotels, and dining cars along the Santa Fe Railway. The Fred Harvey companies also advertised heavily in the *Territorial Enterprise*. Holloway collection

The authors were generally well accepted in Virginia City. "Mary Andreasen and her husband Earl ran the Sazerac Saloon, a favored Beebe luncheon spot. 'We never thought about them being a gay couple,' Mary says today [1992]. 'The town wasn't too fussed about them. They did a lot of good things for the town—Lucius gave the town a fire engine. Whether or not they were gay was never a topic of conversation. Nobody cared about that sort of thing,'"[31] Andria Daley wrote.

The new line of Beebe-Clegg books tapped the nostalgia market. Publishing moved to Howell-North Books of Berkeley, California. *Steamcars to the Comstock* (1957) was followed by nine others, plus reprints of *Mixed Train Daily*. Beebe and Clegg became major stockholders in Howell-North.

Clegg and Beebe purchased a second home in 1957 in Hillsborough, California, south of San Francisco, and they spent winters there. For tax purposes they maintained their legal residence in Virginia City, where they lived in the summers. Nevada did not have a state income tax or inheritance tax.

Their interest in elegance extended to automobiles, especially Rolls-Royces and Bentleys. Beebe owned five Rolls-Royces over his lifetime plus a Jaguar for Clegg. They avoided these models when going on rail photography journeys and rented Buicks or Oldsmobiles instead.[32]

They sold a third of their interest in the *Enterprise* in August 1960 to Roy Shelter, who owned the historic part of the Enterprise Building, with a provision that their names remain on the masthead. A rare Clegg outburst came in 1965, when he complained that the editor was giving Beebe more than his share of credit, saying he (Clegg) was being "relegated ... to the dust bin." He continued, "I very much resent having the success of something over which I dreamed and labored long and hard being credited to only one person when it was factually a very mutual effort."[33]

T-Bone Towser died in November 1960. Beebe's only public displays of affection had been lavished on the St. Bernard, not Clegg. His successor, T-Bone Towser II outlived Beebe and died in 1970.

Beebe began writing his column, "This Wild West," in the *San Francisco Chronicle* in 1960, "eager to do battle with the entrenched forces of liberalism and progress."[34] Like an old western gunfighter, he levied verbal barrages at such institutions as the airline industry, writing that "they have rejected all pretensions to service, comfort, agreeable surroundings, or acceptable company in transit,"[35] and even his own newspaper with statements like, "The *Chronicle* is getting an increasing name for being allied editorially with outright subversion and, by entirely responsible citizens, is openly mentioned as a Communist front newspaper."[36]

He and Clegg churned out books at a brisk pace. The six years beginning in 1960 saw Beebe publish five books with Clegg and an additional six by himself. Beebe proved to be a good picture editor, perhaps better at judging other photographers'

As a part of their promotion for *Cable Car Carnival* in 1951, Beebe and Clegg arranged for San Francisco Mayor Elmer E. Robinson to present them with keys to the city. The book's publication coincided with the city's commitment to maintain cable car service. California State Railroad Museum, BCP1080

Beebe and Clegg's cars stand in front of their winter home in Hillsborough, a wealthy community seventeen miles south of San Francisco. Holloway collection

work than his own. He and Clegg featured such creative photographers as Richard Steinheimer, Robert Hale, Phil Hastings, and Jim Shaughnessy.

Beebe's health declined in the 1960s as his lifestyle of excesses caught up with him. Too much of the best food and drink was actually too much, and he was beset by liver and kidney ailments and attacks of gout. In a letter to David P. Morgan, editor of *Trains,* he complained about a hospital visit "where the most expensive and learned butchers took all my insides out and laid them on the floor, then walked back and forth across them for some hours in prayerful and enquiring mind and, finally stuffed some of them back and sewed them up."[37]

More importantly, as he recovered, he described his publication goals to Morgan. He had always intended, Beebe told Morgan, that his books display a largely pictorial aspect of America. "You have always been aware of my long objective to place the cars and engines in the national picture and not as the special property of the nuts and bolts psychopaths whose suffrage I fear I do not enjoy because somewhere in the middle eighties [a reference to his writings about the 1880s] I misidentified a builder's number from Baldwin or miscalled a wheel arrangement."

Beebe charmed another prominent railroad president, John W. Barriger III (1899–1976) of the Pittsburgh & Lake Erie, into becoming a patron. The railroad purchased books for special occasions and holiday gifts. For the 550 copies of *Great Railroad Photographs,* a line drawing of the P&LE offices appeared on an insert page with the signatures of the two authors.[38] But Beebe turned down freight train shots unless they were completely unavoidable.[39] And he admitted he "was not above faking if the fake is as good as or better than the original."[40] Beebe and Clegg retained lifelong friendships with Barriger and Alfred W. Perlman, who had helped them with their famous narrow gauge tour of Colorado in 1946.

Their prodigious output continued until Beebe's death from heart failure on February 4, 1966, in Hillsborough. Clegg tried to revive him but was unable to do so. In conformity with the times, Clegg could not be listed as a survivor in obituaries, although everyone who knew Beebe, and many who did not, were aware of Clegg's partnership status.

Tributes poured in from across the country. In a front-page story, his former employer, the *Herald Tribune,* described him as "dandy, gourmet, a foremost historian of the American railroad and for many years chronicler of New York's Café Society."[41] Next to the story, Beebe's own obituary, written several years earlier, appeared. It lacked his usual florid prose. Articles also appeared in the *New York Times*[42] and *San Francisco Chronicle*,[43] among others. *Time* magazine was sarcastic.[44]

Morgan, editor of *Trains*, wrote that "at long, long last, we could depart the desert of dust-dry purely educational texts and histories" and acknowledged Beebe as "the man who would enthrall the largest book audience for more than a quarter of a century."[45]

After a funeral in San Francisco, Beebe was cremated. A memorial service was held in Boston and his ashes buried in the Beebe family plot in Wakefield, Massachusetts.[46] Clegg received most of the $2 million estate including assets in Nevada Alvarado Corporation, created by Beebe in 1965 to

"Gentlemen Chefs," looking out of a dining car window, are from left, Andrew Fontes, Clegg, Gilbert Kneiss, Art Colou, Roy Burns, and Beebe. California State Railroad Museum

Clegg (right) and Frank Rapp ride the last westbound *California Zephyr* in 1970. Frank Rapp collection

protect his literary endeavors. Beebe was president, Clegg, vice president. When Beebe died, Clegg became president and Edward S. Colletti, owner of the Delta Saloon and Cafe from 1946 to 1969, vice president. Clegg dissolved the corporation in 1977.

Herb Caen, the *Chronicle* columnist, published Beebe's autobiographical assessment, sent to Caen six years earlier, which contrasted sharply with the self-written obituary.[47] "If anything is worth doing, it's worth doing in style. And on your own terms and nobody's goddamned else's. I like nice clothes because they are an item in an overall facade. In themselves they are silly and foppish. I like big houses and hotel suites and a big dog because they become me. Not for ostentation, but because they give me personal pleasure and satisfaction. ... I take leave of you with an aphorism of the late Michael Arlen, in a way too a Renaissance Man, although he only did one thing well and that only once: 'I require very little of life. I want only the best of everything, and there's so little of that.'"

Windsor French, a society reporter in Cleveland, predicted that "Beebe's books on railroads and trains in the grand luxe were something else and will surely be collected as long as there is a railroad buff alive."[48]

Clegg had work to finish. Howell-North published the second volume of *The Trains We Rode*, eighty percent complete at Beebe's death. Doubleday released Beebe's last book, *The Big Spenders*.

Two compendiums published after Beebe's death acknowledged his literary contributions. Clegg with Duncan Emrich presented a selection of Beebe's writings in *The Lucius Beebe Reader*. Clegg concluded his six-page remembrances in the foreword with these words: "This was the Lucius Beebe I knew and somewhat worshiped."[49]

The *San Francisco Chronicle* published a selection of Beebe's columns.[50] In an introduction, Scott Newhall, executive editor of the *Chronicle*, expressed appreciation to the de Young family, owners of the paper, for tolerating Beebe's "fulminations" for almost six years and acknowledged "their courage in championing this unpredictable genius of American letters."[51]

Clegg recalled that Beebe had been arrested on the steps of the Library of Congress for trying to "liberate" a copy of his book, *Corydon and Other Poems* (1924), written when he was nineteen. Beebe considered it "juvenile trash," although it complained of "no more forests to slash and dismember" fifty years before environmentalism was popular.[52]

Clegg helped care for his mother, Ruth Standish Clegg, as her health declined. She had her own suite in the house in Hillsborough which was decorated with her artwork and had space for her piano. She died in Reno in 1972.[53] Chuck, his sister Ann, and other family members traveled to Memphis to inter her ashes in the Standish family plot.

Clegg sold the Virginia City home in 1979, still keeping legal residence in Nevada, but living in Hillsborough. He continued to make improvements to the railroad car, the *Virginia City*, installing a generator to furnish electric heat in cold weather and operate the air conditioner in summer. His greenhouse at Hillsborough was full of many different varieties of geraniums and he set up an elaborate watering system for the grounds.

Clegg and Frank Rapp, a Western Pacific locomotive engineer living in Oakland, developed a friendship that began around 1966 and lasted until Clegg's death. Rapp assisted with the maintenance of the *Virginia City*. He recalls many pleasant dinners with Clegg on Thursday nights, when his housekeeper, Mrs. Catherine Begger, had the day off. Rapp and Clegg traveled twice to Central City, Colorado, for the opera festival and once to Europe about 1972, going to restaurants and hotels in London and Paris that Clegg and Beebe had visited earlier and traveling on the *Blue Train* to Monte Carlo. Rapp remembers Clegg as "very nice and very polite and quite a gentleman. If he said he was going to do something, he would do it. He

Beebe and Clegg at a party at their home in Virginia City, which they called the John Piper House. California State Railroad Museum, BCP1128

never disappointed me in his entire life." After retiring from Union Pacific in 2010, Rapp and his wife moved to the Palm Springs area.[54]

Clegg suffered from an inner-ear disorder called Meniere's disease, which he learned to control through his diet. He was health-conscious and ate small portions. He wrote two diet cookbooks which were never published because the recipes were based on a controversial artificial sweetener. Rapp said, "Chuck told me that when Lucius found out he was being served diet food, Lucius joked that he would eat twice as much."

Charles Clegg took his own life on August 25, 1979. He gave no indications of his intentions, but the date was significant. Both Chuck and Lucius lived exactly 23,069 days—not a coincidence, but a testament to the immense bond between the two.

His sister, Ann Clegg Holloway, and her husband, John, immediately flew to San Francisco to handle arrangements; their children came a day or two later. His brother, Myles S. Clegg of Seekonk,

Massachusetts, also survived him. Funeral services were held at a Burlingame mortuary.[55] Alfred Perlman, who had recently retired as Western Pacific chairman, was at the wake. Clegg's ashes were buried in the Clegg family plot in Youngstown, Ohio, along with ashes from Beebe, T-Bone Towser I, and T-Bone Towser II. Mrs. Holloway received the bulk of the estate including literary rights. She and her husband retained ties to Virginia City; they built a house, designed by their son Peter, on the foundations of the swimming pool next to the Beebe-Clegg home.

In their professional lives, Beebe and Clegg began by showcasing their own heroic images of trains, moving creatively ahead with pictures and texts, reaching a peak in *Mixed Train Daily*. They went on to recognize other venues and photographers, giving increased attention to railroad imagery, culminating in *Great Railroad Photographs U.S.A.* Their last book, the two-volume epic, *The Trains We Rode,* was a fitting conclusion to their publishing ventures.

Their openly gay lifestyle, at a time when it was not generally accepted outside New York City's upper crust, did not seem to interfere with their ability to obtain cooperation from railroad officials, promotional support from the news media, or profitable book sales. This is a part of their story that only now can be discussed freely, but has yet to be fully explored in the contexts of their friendships and associations, which is beyond the scope of this book.

It is time to take a new look at their photos, which is the point of this work. Today's design and printing techniques provide an opportunity to reevaluate their prolific output and make their work shine as never before.

Beebe and Clegg were the right people for their time. Now, the time is right to celebrate and examine their contributions to railroad history and the historical record. They pioneered the genre of railroad books, brought their material to mass-market audiences, and established themselves as household names. Their work built the foundation for continuing interest in creative railroad photography and helped aggrandize shortline and narrow-gauge railroading.

Come with us as we explore these ideas and present Lucius Beebe and Charles Clegg's most memorable images—unsurpassed in their dedication to elegance and everyday railroading. Together, they elevated the railroad to an icon of the American experience.

Beebe and Clegg's own words in *Age of Steam: A Classic Album of American Railroading* best describe their admiration for railroads and locomotives: "For fifteen decades 'the tall, far-trafficking shapes' of American record were the smoke plumes of burning wood, coal, and oil that moved with compulsive majesty across the summer horizons of a nation bound on mighty landfarings. They were the tangible symbols and oriflamme of a universal preoccupation with movement and the realization of a continental dimension."[56]

Notes

1. Herb Caen, "Beebe on Beebe," *San Francisco Chronicle*, Feb. 13, 1966.
2. Robert Selph Henry, *Trains* (Indianapolis: The Bobbs-Merrill Company, 1934 and 1938).
3. Two of Clegg's friends, Frank Rapp and Michael McCreary, confirmed the name. For background, see Anthony Summers, *Official and Confidential: The Secret Life of J. Edgar Hoover* (New York, N.Y.: G. P. Putnam's Sons, 1993).
4. Charles Clegg, Foreword, 11, to *The Lucius Beebe Reader,* selected and edited by Clegg and Duncan Emrich. (Garden City, NY: Doubleday & Co., 1967).
5. Clegg, Foreword, 11.
6. Woodcut, *Rio Grande: Main Line of the Rockies,* p. 22, is from *Harper's Weekly,* July 17, 1875.
7. Ann Clegg Holloway, interview with John Gruber and John Ryan, June 23, 2015, Washington, D.C.
8. Michael McCreary, interview with Gruber and Ryan,

Beebe stands next to his first Rolls-Royce, a 1938 Phantom III town limousine by Brewster-Inskip he purchased in 1952, with their home in Virginia City in the background. Beebe signed the print, "To Grahame," who is Grahame Hardy, publisher of early Beebe-Clegg books: *Virginia & Truckee, Legends of the Comstock Lode,* and *Cable Car Carnival.* California State Railroad Museum, BCP0089

April 15, 2016, Trump National Golf Club, Rancho Palos Verdes, Calif.

9. Jerome Zerbe, Diary, April 23, 1942. Jerome Zerbe Photographs and Papers. General Collection, Beinecke Rare Book and Manuscript Library, Yale University.

10. "One-Man U.S.O.," in *Snoot If You Must* (New York, London: D. Appleton-Century Co., 1943), 230–244.

11. Report of Changes, U.S. Navy Muster Rolls, 1943. National Archives at College Park, from ancestry.com.

12. Clegg Naval Record, National Personnel Records Center, National Archives, St. Louis, Mo. The memos are mentioned but do not appear in Clegg's record.

13. "Gotham's Guide for Good-Time Charlies," *American Weekly,* June 11, 1944.

14. Freeman Hubbard, "Interesting Railfans no. 62, *Railroad,* Feb. 1968, 20.

15. Bennett Cerf, *Try and Stop Me: A Collection of Anecdotes and Stories, Mostly Humorous* (New York: Simon and Schuster, 1944), 143–144.

16. "Golden Spike," Voice of the Army, April 14, 1947. Peter Holloway collection.

17. "It Takes More Than Speed," Graflex, similar ads in *Commercial Photographer,* March 1946, and *U.S. Camera,* April 1946.

18. Hubbard, 23.

19. Beebe with Clegg, *Mixed Train Daily* (New York: E. P. Dutton & Co., 1947), 3.

20. Pasquale Marranzino, "Author and Notables Ride Narrow Gauge as in '90s," *Rocky Mountain News,* Oct. 1, 1946. See also Oct. 2–5, 1946.

21. "*Life* Goes to a Party," *Life,* Oct. 13, 1947, 160–164.

22. Ann Clegg Holloway, interview with John Gruber, Virginia City, Nev., Sept. 12, 2013.

23. "Private Railroad Cars Are Almost Extinct, Alas," *Life,* Dec. 20, 1948.

24. Alma Dettinger Show, WQRX, Dec. 22, 1949. Peter Holloway collection.

25. Managing Editor George A. Cornish to Beebe, March 8, 1950, Holloway collection.

26. Beebe, "I Saw the Elephant," *Holiday,* September 1950, 76.

27. Andria Daley, "Boardwalk Bons Vivants," *Nevada,* Nov.–Dec. 1992, 22.

28. Karl Breckenridge, "Breck: Lucius Beebe, Charles Clegg and the T-Bone Towsers," *Reno Gazette-Journal,* Jan. 22, 2016.

29. "Last Private Car Brings National Fame To Virginia City," *Territorial Enterprise* 103, no. 11, March 16, 1956.

30. "Beebe Rolls East in Rail Splendor," *New York Times,* Feb. 23, 1956, 29.

31. Daley, 35.

32. Documentation preserved by Michael McCreary.

33. Clegg to Lew Harvey, *Territorial Enterprise,* Dec. 15, 1965, Holloway Collection.

34. Gordon Pates, *Introduction, Provocative Pen of Lucius Beebe, Esq. (*San Francisco: Chronicle Publishing Co., 1966), viii.

35. "No Carriage Trade for the Airlines," *The Provocative Pen,* 211.

36. Scott Newhall, "Lucius Beebe of The Chronicle," *Chronicle,* Feb. 7, 1966.

37. Beebe to David P. Morgan, Nov. 21, 1962, David P. Morgan Library, Kalmbach Publishing Co.

38. Beebe to Barriger, March 10, 1964, Barriger Library.

39. Beebe to Barriger, received Feb. 7, 1964, Barriger Library.

40. Beebe to Barriger, Jan. 24, 1962, Barriger Library.

41. Don Ross. "Legendary Lucius Beebe Dies—Olden Elegance at Any Cost," *Herald Tribune,* Feb. 5, 1966.

42. "Lucius Beebe, Newspaper Columnist, Author and Bon Vivant, Dies at 63," *New York Times,* Feb. 5, 1966 (from Associated Press).

43. Ron Fimrite, "Lucius Beebe is Dead." *Chronicle*, Feb. 5, 1966, 1, 8.

44. Milestones, *Time,* Feb. 11, 1966, 82.

45. David P. Morgan, "Lucius Morris Beebe, 1902–1966," *Trains,* April 1966.

46. "Lucius Beebe Funeral Rites, *Boston (Mass.) Herald,* Feb. 6, 1966.

47. Herb Caen, "Beebe on Beebe," *San Francisco Chronicle,* Feb. 13, 1966.

48. Windsor French, *Cleveland Press,* Feb. 25, 1966, 3.

49. Clegg, Foreword to *The Lucius Beebe Reader,* selected and edited by Clegg and Duncan Emrich (Garden City, NY: Doubleday & Co., 1967), 14.

50. *The Provocative Pen of Lucius Beebe, Esq. (*San Francisco: Chronicle Publishing Co., 1966).

51. Scott Newhall, "Some Words of Appreciation," *The Provocative Pen of Lucius Beebe.*

52. Clegg, "Quid Restat?" undated, Peter Holloway collection.

53. "Ruth S. Clegg," *Reno Gazette-Journal,* Dec. 9, 1972.

54. Frank Rapp, interview with John Gruber, July 10, 2015.

55. "Author Charles Clegg, 63, Found Dead," *San Mateo Times,* Aug. 27, 1979.

56. Beebe and Clegg, Foreword, *The Age of Steam* (New York, Toronto: Rinehart & Co., 1957), 8.

Beebe and Clegg's *Gold Coast* includes a fireplace in its interior (top). In March 1980 it stands in Sacramento lettered "Central of Georgia" for use in a political campaign scene in a movie. When moved inside for permanent display, it was relettered "Georgia Northern." Photos by Shirley Burman, California State Railroad Museum

Their Cameras, by Mel Patrick

Beebe's first railroad book, *High Iron*, published in 1938, contained many of his own photographs. His camera of choice, as noted in *Trains* magazine's first issue, dated November 1940, was the Graflex model D equipped with a Zeiss f/3.5 lens. This was a single lens reflex camera with the 4" by 5" version made between 1927 and 1947 by the Folmer-Graflex Co. (formerly the Folmer and Schwing Department of Eastman Kodak), and it is this model of camera that is seen in the hands of author Beebe shown on the dust jacket of *High Iron* and *Highball*.

The Graflex model D had the advantage of flash capability, although no photograph by Beebe with a flash is known to exist. Beebe also used an earlier Graflex model B which lacked flash capability, and it is this model of the Graflex that appears in photos of Beebe taken by Clegg beginning in 1944. At some point after the completion of *Mixed Train Daily*, Beebe used a Speed Graphic, probably the Anniversary Speed Graphic all-black wartime model, made between 1940 and 1947. All of Beebe's cameras were equipped with a 4" by 5" sheet film back, allowing use of sheet film packs that could quickly move the next sheet of unexposed film into place; Beebe states in the November 1940 *Trains* that he used Kodak Super XX film, originally rated at ASA 100.

Clegg joined Beebe in railroad photography in 1944 using a Kodak Medalist (made between 1941 and 1948), equipped with a Kodak Ektar 100mm f/3.5 five element fixed lens and using size 620 film producing 2¼" by 3¼" negatives. After the war, Clegg acquired a second Medalist, the model 2 (made between 1946 and 1953), with coated lenses

Beebe with his camera in 1937 at Georgetown, Colorado. Photo by Jerome Zerbe, Jerome Zerbe Photographs and Papers. General Collection, Beinecke Rare Book and Manuscript Library, © 2018, Yale University

and synced flash capability. The Kodak Medalist cameras were known as possibly the all-time best American-made camera.

In almost all cases, Beebe was using a 4" by 5" size camera and Clegg was using the smaller roll-film Medalist. But that was not always the case: there are two known examples of Beebe using a Medalist and one of Clegg having used a 4" by 5."

While holding his Graflex model B camera, Beebe makes a detailed view of no. 5, the wood burning yard engine of the Brooks-Scanlon Lumber Co. at Foley, Florida. Brooks-Scanlon and its Live Oak, Perry & Gulf Railroad are covered in *MTD*, pages 8–13, but without the photo of Beebe (facing page). Clegg, California State Railroad Museum, BC2400

Champagne Salute at Promontory

In 1949 Beebe and Clegg reenacted the golden spike ceremony at Promontory, Utah, for the eightieth anniversary of the completion of the Transcontinental Railroad. They posed with spike mauls and then raised their glasses in a champagne toast to the driving of the golden spike on May 10, 1869. The third person is Owen V. Gibson (1905–1958), Southern Pacific passenger agent, Ogden. The toast was entirely appropriate, since the famous Andrew J. Russell photo of the 1869 ceremony shows the workers holding a bottle of champagne. Today, the location is a part of the Golden Spike National Historic Site. The obelisk, built in 1916 by the Southern Pacific, stood alone in the desolate landscape in 1949. The National Park Service moved it to a new location next to the visitor center in 2004. The recessed granite plaque was covered with concrete and a bronze plaque placed over the original plaque. John D. Eccles photos, California State Railroad Museum, BCP1116, BCP1117

2 Beebe and the Beginnings

Young Lucius Beebe relished a fun-filled life, with experiences ranging from serious academic studies at prestigious universities to pranks in the countryside. Among the not-so-serious activities of Boy Beebe: blowing up outhouses. Beebe led an unconventional lifestyle almost from the beginning. A tall person, at six feet, four inches, he presented an imposing image.

Lucius Morris Beebe, born into a wealthy Boston family on December 9, 1902, used his social status to advance his interests in writing, railroading, and photography. He was the fourth child of Junius Beebe (1854–1934) and Eleanor Harriett Merrick Beebe (1865–1939). Other children were Lucia Beebe Rockwood (1892–1963), Junius Oliver Beebe (1894–1933), and Junius Merrick Beebe (1891–1892). Junius Oliver died while making his first solo airplane flight, which fueled Lucius's dislike of flying.

The family summered on Beebe Farm, a 140-acre holding in Wakefield, Massachusetts, where Beebe was born. The remainder of the year was spent at their residence at 96 Bay State Road in Boston. Junius Beebe, a banker and leather merchant, had a variety of investments that stretched from Wakefield and Boston clear across the country to orchards in Washington. He was also a director of the Mexican Northern Railway & Mining Company and the Piney River & Paint Creek (leased to Virginian Railway, 1912) and the White Oak (leased to C&O and Virginian, 1912) Railways in West Virginia.[1] The *National Cyclopaedia of American Biography* contains a full list of his business interests.[2] His wife, Eleanor, was the daughter of John Mudge Merrick, professor of chemistry at Harvard. Junius donated funds for the Lucius Beebe Library in Wakefield, named for his father, Lucius Morris's namesake.

While attending the North Ward public school in Wakefield, the younger Lucius spent his free time engaged in activities such as visiting relatives and reading the comics section of the Sunday newspaper. He also enjoyed watching trains. He and a school friend, Arthur Sawyer, who lived at the Lenox Hotel overlooking the Boston & Albany coach yards in Boston, spent "long afternoons in all seasons and weather leaning perilously over grimy window sills and becoming sootier by the moment watching the Boston sections of the *Lake Shore Limited* and *Wolverine* being made up for their long runs into the western sunset."[3]

All appearance of innocence vanished at age twelve, when Lucius became a "confirmed dynamiter." Dennis Daly, the overseer at his father's farm, taught him about dynamite. On the evening of July 3, 1914, the target was Farmer Cox's new outhouse, "a three-holer whose convenience and pleasing design had aroused general admiration." Beebe and a friend traveled to the location in a horse and buggy. Beebe placed the dynamite but miscalculated the time for the fuse to set it off. The "welcoming salute to Independence Day" exploded at about the time Beebe got back to the buggy. The horse bolted, returning to the stable alone. "No concealment of such a debacle seemed practical," Beebe wrote. Two days later he was dispatched to a summer camp in Maine, "famous for its "Dannemora discipline," referring to a New York state prison in the community of Dannemora.[4]

In rapid succession, two Massachusetts prep schools sent him home: St. Marks of Southboro for another dynamiting episode, and Berkshire School of Sheffield for Lucius's discovery of alcohol. He finished Roxbury School of Cheshire, Connecticut,

In the beginning days of his photography, Beebe championed the three-quarters or wedge-of-pie view of the side and full length of the train. An outstanding example shows the streamliner, *City of San Francisco,* heading east from Ogden, Utah, in 1939. The train is near East Riverdale Yard; Mount Ben Lomand dominates the skyline. "On the Wings of the Morning" is no. 40 in his second book, *Highliners: A Railroad Album.* What Beebe photographed that day was the fourteen-car, second-generation trainset dedicated to Chicago-Oakland/San Francisco service, extra-fare with a 39¾ hour schedule. This is the trainset that derailed in Nevada west of Palisade on August 12, 1939, killing two dozen passengers and crew (after which majority opinion favored malicious sabotage as the cause, rather than negligence). Beebe, California State Railroad Museum, BC0807

Lucius Beebe with his grandmother at Beebe Farm, Wakefield, about October 1904. Holloway collection

and entered Yale in 1922. A prank involving a professor in the Divinity School led to his dismissal in the middle of his sophomore year.

In a move that would set the stage for the rest of his life, he then spent a year as a newspaper reporter for the *Boston Telegram*. After that, he enrolled in Harvard where, despite a short suspension, he received a bachelor of arts degree mid-term in 1928. He spent another year at Harvard studying the poetry of Edward Arlington Robinson, then abandoned academic life and took his second newspaper job with the *Boston Evening Transcript* as a contributor to its literary section.[5]

Beebe moved to New York in June 1929, accepting a job with the *New York Herald Tribune*, which was owned by heirs of mining, banking, and railroad ventures associated with the Comstock Lode and San Francisco, two topics which would later fascinate Beebe. The *Herald Tribune*'s city editor, Stanley Walker, who hired Beebe at $35 a week, had never seen a reporter "of such baroque design." He relegated Beebe to general assignments for the next four years.

"Thus began a career which may be tritely described as unique in American journalism, although it can never be said that Mr. Beebe was much of a reporter," Wolcott Gibbs wrote in his famous *New Yorker* profile. "He had an apathy about facts which verged closely on actual dislike, and the tangled wildwood of his prose was poorly adapted to describing small fires and negligible thefts."[6]

Beebe lived in a two-room suite in the Madison Hotel, where he received a reduced rate because the hotel wanted to list prestigious clientele among its residents. He was never above pinching pennies.

He made it a habit to be at the opening night of the summer festival season at the elegant Central City (Colorado) Opera House. In 1932, actress Lillian Gish opened the newly restored opera house with *Camille*, launching the annual festival tradition. Beebe wrote that the event "set all Colorado by the ears."[7] He frequently met Evalyn Walsh McLean, daughter of a multimillionaire miner who came from Washington, D.C., and they socialized in Colorado and Washington often.

Test-marketing for a new Beebe column started in 1933, with "So This Is New York" in the *Philadelphia Inquirer* and "New York Speaking" elsewhere. Satisfied with the response, the *Herald Tribune* introduced the Saturday morning column on June 2, 1934, as "This New York."

The column brought Manhattan's Café Society into "open glory" and delighted readers, according to Gibbs, who said that Beebe's "general definition of Café Society" was it "might be an unorganized but generally recognized group of persons who participate in the professional and social life of New York available to those possessed of a certain degree of affluence and manners.'" This was Beebe's mission until 1944.[8]

Besides his newspaper reporting, Beebe maintained an aggressive writing schedule. He contributed the introduction to Jerome Zerbe's *People on Parade* (1934). In it, Beebe described Zerbe's photos as "news pictures of a highly specialized sort showing elegant or famous or witty people in brief instants of parade and pleasure."[9] Zerbe was the official photographer of Manhattan's nightspot El Morocco; he also was in a relationship with Beebe. Zerbe's New York photos of Beebe appear in *Happy Times* (1973, with text by Brendan Gill).

The column and his affiliation with Zerbe brought attention of another sort. Beebe was parodied as "Doc. Beebe" in W. C. Fields's film *You're Telling Me* (Paramount, 1934). Another society columnist, Walter Winchell of Hearst's *Daily Mirror*, derisively referred to Beebe as "Luscious Lucius."

Beebe's father Junius died the same year that the Fields film appeared. The relationship between Beebe and his father had been tested often, and the newspaper column would seem to have been an element of success that the senior Beebe could take pride in. Lucius saw fit to take his father to Bleeck's Artists & Writers Club, the *Herald Tribune*'s favored watering hole. There was only one such visit. His father asked about "two burlesque figures" in the corner of the bar. Lucius identified them as Ogden Reid, publisher of the *Herald Tribune*, and Reid's cousin, Ogden Mills, secretary of the U.S. Treasury. "Father took the *Owl* home on the New Haven and was never the same afterward."[10] In fact, he died not long after of a heart attack at Pennsylvania Station in New York City.

In 1935 Appleton-Century released *Boston and the Boston Legend*, dedicated to the memory of his father, Junius. Beebe's eleven-page chapter about railroads, "Highball and Johnson Bar," recognized that a gravity system serving a granite quarry in 1804 was the first railroad in the United States. A Johnson Bar is the reverse lever on a steam locomotive, and a Highball is a historic railroad signal which allows a train to proceed if the ball is at the top of a pole. The book thus showed that he had mastered railroad jargon. It set the stage for his railroad writing for the next quarter of a century.[11]

Beebe told Ernie Pyle, a columnist for the Scripps-Howard newspapers, that writing about railroads for the Boston book had turned him into a railfan. Pyle went on to quote a critique by Beebe of railfans: "He says they're divided into a dozen separate groups, such as narrow-gauge fans, steam-engine fans, diesel fans, live-photography fan, still-photography fans, and so on. He says all hate each other and a fan of one group won't speak to a fan of another group." Beebe placed himself in the live-photography group.[12]

Beebe's flamboyant attire was a key component of his public image. When the Merchant Tailors' Designers Association listed him in 1937 among the sixteen best-dressed men in the U.S., it described him as "the greatest dandy of his time, a perfectionist in dress." Also in the list was President Franklin D. Roosevelt.[13] Beebe made the association's honor roll in 1939 for "restoring elegance to men's clothes, particularly with reference to the mink-lined overcoat with astrakhan collar."[14]

In interviews in *Railroad* magazine and Appleton-Century's *Book Chat*,[15] Beebe confirmed that he took up photography because of the lack of suitable photographs for publication. It was the "terrible-tempered Mrs. Haskell," senior editor at Appleton-Century, who suggested that he produce a picture book on railroading, and further challenged him to make his own pictures for the book. He poked fun at Elizabeth Haskell's dress and appearance, and yet they conducted regular "devotions of the muse" of alcohol at the McAlpin Hotel bar in New York and came to agreements about the book.[16] Appleton-Century published his next four railroad books.

Beebe obviously took advantage of a *Herald Tribune* connection. Her husband, William E. Haskell, Jr., was assistant to the publisher. After

Lucius Beebe, about three years old, at Beebe Farm, Wakefield. Holloway collection

leaving Appleton-Century, Mrs. Haskell (1900–1961) served as director of student personnel at Bennington College.[17]

Although Beebe did discuss his Graflex camera (See "Their Cameras," page 33, by Mel Patrick), he never explained where and how he learned to take pictures. It is very likely that a combination of factors schooled him in photography: observation of friends, companions, and colleagues who took pictures; examination of photographs as a writer, editor, reader; conversations with photographers and editors; and personal experiments with photography. He probably learned to write in much the same informal way.

His first train book was barely underway when the flattering two-part *New Yorker* profile appeared in 1937. Wolcott Gibbs devoted only a paragraph to Beebe and railroads: "This is not the unaccountable enterprise it might seem at first, because he has chosen to regard steam locomotives like the hansoms at the Plaza, as symbols of the polite and vanishing past." Gibbs recognized Beebe was an authority on railroading, citing his 1936 appearance at "Parade of Years" in Cleveland where he operated locomotives on the exposition's private tracks.

Beebe's book, *High Iron: A Book of Trains* (1938), won a new audience for railroad photography. Beebe himself took the majority of its 174 photographs. Freeman Hubbard, editor of *Railroad* magazine, in "Interesting Railfans: 3" wrote, "Many of his camera studies are quite good." Beebe later recalled that it was "a crude thing by present-day standards, but it seemed to touch off a lot of other railroad books."[18] David P. Morgan, *Trains* editor, disagreed. Morgan told Beebe: "I suppose at heart I'll never get over the thrill of being an eleven-

40 Beebe & Clegg: Their Enduring Photographic Legacy

year-old recipient of a copy of *High Iron,* which my Dad purchased for the enormous price (in 1938) of $5. You certainly shook up the book trade then, and happily, still are."[19]

The happy success of *High Iron* provided impetus for future book ventures, which are described in more detail in later chapters.

Beebe's commitment to railroad history grew when he joined the Railway & Locomotive Historical Society in 1938. He upgraded to life membership around 1958. At the time of the upgrade, Clegg was also an annual member.[20] Beebe continued to gain recognition for his social achievements, which also boosted his appeal as a railroad conductor and industry ambassador.

Known for his dashing style, he appeared on a 1939 *Life* magazine cover for his trendy use of men's jewelry. "Modish Men Revive Chains and Rings and Jewelry Sales Reach a New High," the headline said. *Life* included a picture of Beebe's railroad watch ($62.50) and gold chain ($175).[21]

Beebe made the *Chicago Tribune* gossip pages while he was in Chicago in 1939 to photograph the Rock Island Railroad for his second train book. Columnist June Provines talked with him at a cocktail party. "There are as many rules governing the photographing of trains as there are about the classic French drama," she quoted him as saying. He asserted that ideal photos "should include country typical of the run and smoke trails to indicate motion." Provines concluded that Beebe failed to live up to his reputation for elegant grooming, including a habitual diamond gardenia brooch for his lapel. "It is only fair to add that the three times we saw Mr. Beebe he was drinking and not eating, the diamond gardenia was not in evidence, he had on the same brown suit, and once he needed a shave," she said.[22] A few weeks later, Beebe was back and set off for Wisconsin to stalk trains with friend Peter Moon of Chicago."[23]

Although he complained it was a "vulgar" question, he described his finances for a reporter in Omaha, where he was taking pictures of the Union Pacific for a book. "I am a single young man of expensive tastes. I spend $25,000 to $50,000 for living," he said. He was on a three-week leave from the *Herald Tribune,* traveling to the Pacific Coast and back. After some "nourishing whiskey" he told about his land holdings: a 140-acre farm north of Boston; 7,000 acres with 75,000 apple trees in the state of Washington; a farm in Minneapolis, now sold; goat farm in Arkansas, until a flood drowned the goats; and a garage in Key West, "in which no car has ever been parked."[24]

Beebe never missed a promotional opportunity. He wrote about Southern Pacific's Sparks-to-Oakland Sunday local for the preview and volume one, number one, issues of *Trains,* plus "Railroad Photography" for issue number one. "Patience, planning, and eye to detail are needed to get satisfactory action shots of trains," he told readers. Two photos appeared in the issue. Contributions by Beebe continued and by issue five of *Trains* he rated the cover.

Beebe as a young man in 1931. Holloway collection

Beebe at the bar in his Madison Hotel suite in New York City. Photo by Jerome Zerbe, Holloway collection

In his role as a Hollywood consultant, he raked in cash and furthered his notoriety. When he arrived in Los Angeles to serve as technical adviser for Paramount's *Union Pacific* (1939), starring Barbara Stanwyck and Joel McCrea, UP President William M. Jeffers let him take the throttle and bring the streamlined *City of Los Angeles* into the station. (Beebe would dedicate his second book to Jeffers.)

"While the train's regular engineer stood by, Beebe—in a black homburg hat, black braided morning coat, Ascot tie, shepherd's check trousers, white waistcoat, and stiff-bosomed shirt—performed the feat with considerable distinction," Yvone Jean Stephens wrote about Beebe in her doctoral dissertation at the University of Iowa.[25]

Beebe got the adviser's job, according to a profile in *American Mercury,* "principally because his hobby, and a good clean one it is too, is photographing and collecting legends of railroading, which Beebe honestly calls his 'secret lunacy.'"[26]

Union Pacific and the city of Omaha staged a three-day celebration for the premiere of the film, with special trains from Chicago and the Pacific Coast. Beebe covered the events in a story headlined "Yip-Yipping Celebration in Frontier Costume Takes Over Town for New Film."[27]

Likewise, in St. Louis Beebe piloted a special train of two coaches through a ribbon, dedicating an interlocking tower at St. Louis Union Station. The ceremony, under the auspices of the Terminal Railroad Association of St. Louis, included lunch in the private dining room at the station. The association's general counsel presented Beebe with a certificate designating him "Railroad Enthusiast No. 1." In accepting the award and a silver cocktail set, Beebe expressed the hope that "the honor that was paid him would bring recognition to all amateur railroaders who play a great part in establishing a feeling of good will toward all railroads."[28]

Beebe served as technical adviser for the Paramount film *Café Society,* appearing in the film for four minutes as a publicity person and mentioning his name in a few lines of the dialogue. Paramount paid Beebe $500 for permission to use the title, upsetting Hearst's New York columnist, Maury Paul (writing under the pseudonym, Cholly Knickerbocker), who claimed he had coined the term in 1919.[29]

Beebe made his first visit to Virginia City in 1940 while covering the premier of the film *Virginia City*. He panned the film but applauded Warner Brothers' three-day press party. The company brought a sixteen-car train of film celebrities from Los Angeles for the opening. The countryside "turned out in cowboy regalia and two weeks' whiskers to a man." Private autos and buses, escorted by state police, brought the crowd up the steep Geiger Grade road to Piper's Opera House. But the stars arrived late and Virginia City residents were irate.[30] In additon, the owner of the Virginia Theater, where the film was being shown, had boosted prices and distributed free whiskey with the tickets, resulting in a rowdy crowd. Fearing for their safety, a Warner Brothers official sent the stars back early, further upsetting the townspeople. In the final accounting, Virginia City tabulated $50,000 in bar sales alone.[31]

In 1950, Lucius Beebe set aside any memory of these disappointments and he and his partner Charles Clegg made their home in Virginia City.

Notes

1. *Poor's Manual of Railroads* (New York: H. V. & H. W. Poor, 1913), 518, 523.
2. *National Cyclopaedia of American Biography* 25 (New York: James T. White & Co., 1936), 244.
3. Beebe, "Metropolis with Manners," in Charles Clegg and Duncan Emrich, *The Lucius Beebe Reader* (Garden City, NY: Doubleday & Co., 1967), 28.
4. Beebe, "Wakefield, Massachusetts: The Town That Never Will Forget Me," *Lucius Beebe Reader,* 43-44.
5. Duncan Emrich, "Lucius Beebe: A Biographical Sketch." *Lucius Beebe Reader,* 389-390.
6. Wolcott Gibbs, "The Diamond Gardenia—II," *New Yorker,* Nov. 27, 1937.
7. Beebe, "The Ethereal Miss Gash, Delos Chappel, and a New Camille," *New York Herald Tribune*, Oct. 2, 1932.
8. Gibbs, "The Diamond Gardenia—I," *New Yorker,* Nov. 20, 1937.
9. Jerome Zerbe, *People on Parade* (New York: David Kemp, Publisher, 1934), 7.
10. Beebe, "Father Visits Bleeck's," *The Provocative Pen of Lucius Beebe, Esq.* (San Francisco: Chronicle Publishing Co., 1966), 13.
11. Beebe, "Highball and Johnson Bar," *Boston and the Boston Legend* (New York, London: D. Appleton-Century Co., 1936), 131-141.
12. Ernie Pyle, Ravings, *Montana Standard,* July 22, 1941.
13. "Roosevelt Is Among 16 Best-Dressed U.S. Men," *Herald Tribune,* Feb. 9, 1937, 12.
14. "20 Best-Dressed Men In America Are Listed," *Herald Tribune,* Feb. 8, 1939, 20.
15. *Appleton-Century Book Chat,* Dec. 10, 1938, p. 4, quoted in Yvone Jean Stephens (1926–2011), "Lucius Morris Beebe, Seeing the Elephant" (University of Iowa, Ph.D., 1972), 67-68.
16. Beebe, "The Sunny Side of Grubb Street," *Provocative Pen,* 12.
17. "Mrs. W. E. Haskell Jr. of Bennington Dead," *New York Times,* Jan, 27, 1961, 33.
18. "Interesting Railfans no. 3, Lucius Beebe," *Railroad,* August 1961.
19. Kevin P. Keefe, "Lucius & David," *Trains,* Feb. 2011.
20. William F. Howes, Vice-President Member Services, R&LHS, to Gruber, Aug. 1, 2017.
21. "Lucius Beebe Sets a Style," *Life,* Jan. 16, 1939, cover, 42-43.
22. June Provines, "Front Views and Profiles," *Chicago Tribune,* Sept. 23, 1939.
23. Provines, *Chicago Tribune,* Oct. 13, 1939.
24. Robert McGrath, "High-Priced Newsmen Talk About Cost of Living, Need of Nourishment," *Omaha Bee-News,* n.d. Holloway collection.
25. Stephens, "Seeing the Elephant," 70.
26. John Richmond, "Orchidaceous Lucius Beebe, *American Mercury,* Nov. 1940, 317.
27. Beebe, "Omaha Opens 'Union Pacific' As Six-Guns Pop," *Herald Tribune,* April 19, 1939, 10.
28. "St. Louis Station Dedicates Rail Control Tower," *Herald Tribune,* Dec. 1, 1940, 24.
29. Richmond, "Orchidaceous Lucius Beebe, 216.
30. "Comstock Irate Over Premiere Failings," *Reno Gazette-Journal,* March 19, 1940.
31. David Barnett, "Virginia City: The Movie," *Nevada* 50: 5 (Sept.-Oct. 1990, 47.

Life Goes to a Ma & Pa Party

In Beebe and Clegg's biggest public relations coup, the nation's leading pictorial weekly devoted most of four pages to "*Life* Goes to a Party," which celebrated the publication of *Mixed Train Daily*. The event was a rolling party on a mixed train of the Maryland & Pennsylvania, complete with generous amounts of food and free-flowing liquor. Attendees are shown in an open car at Delta, Pennsylvania (facing page). Ann Clegg Holloway, Chuck's sister, enjoyed a visit with the locomotive engineer (above). Holloway collection

Beebe's signature view shows the front of his beloved *Twentieth Century Limited,* the flagship of the New York Central, by industrial designer Henry Dreyfuss. The photo appears in Beebe's first book, *High Iron,* on page 165. Beebe was influenced by Ivan Dmitri when the two collaborated on an article for *Town and County* in 1936. The photos in this chapter are examples of Beebe's Dmitri-inspired views of trains. California State Railroad Museum, BC2543

3 The Visual Influences

Lucius Beebe started publishing railroad photography books at a time when the public was hungry for a quality product: interesting images printed on high quality presses. During the 1930s and 1940s, books and magazines on slick paper were the only game in town. Newspaper reproduction was generally poor, television barely existed, and the internet was unimagined. Facebook, Flickr, and cellphone photography did not exist.

Being business-minded, Beebe doubtless realized that he could make money by moving his interest in railroading into publishing railroad books. Beebe's plumes of blackened smoke, aided by the camera, darkroom, and design talents of Charles Clegg, brought further acclaim for Beebe and public recognition for Clegg.

The 1930s and 1940s were a time of considerable evolution in photojornalism and documentary and pictorial photography. *Fortune,* founded in 1930, featured quality photography. *Life,* begun in 1936, built increasing interest in photo stories generally. *Look,* launched a year later, was a biweekly magazine with a strong emphasis on photography. *Trains* joined the parade of glossy magazines in 1940—with Beebe images in the first issues.

Lewis Hine (1874–1940), who had been making portraits of workers since 1921, brought his style to *Fortune* in 1939 with a pictorial story about Lewis D. Isaac, a Lackawanna Railroad fireman. Horace Bristol (1908–1997) photographed the Southern Railway's Charlotte Division in 1938 for *Life,*[1] with a photograph of Ps-4 Pacific no. 1397. (Editor David P. Morgan later reproduced this image proudly in *Trains.*[2]) Bristol showed the Southern Pacific in color in *Fortune* in 1942[3] and Gordon Coster and Bernard Hoffman created a photo essay about the Rock Island for *Life* in 1946.[4]

Beebe had friends at *Life,* but there is no confirmation of its direct influence on him. *Life* featured Eric Schaal's views of a milk train on the St. Johnsbury & Lake Champlain in Vermont in 1942. "This rattletrap mixed local is a part of rural living in Vermont," penned the unidentified *Life* writer.[5] The article is certainly in the spirit of *Mixed Train Daily,* which covered the same railroad, but Beebe never would have called the train "rattletrap."

Concurrent with railroading's emergence in popular jouranlism, the federal government sponsored several significant photography projects that touched on the topic. In late 1936 the National Research Program of the Works Progress Administration hired Hine as chief photographer. Roy Stryker (1893–1975) famously ran the Farm Security Administration-Office of War Information photo project, the largest documentary enterprise of the twentieth century. FSA photographers, especially Jack Delano, covered railroads extensively.[6]

Despite his frugality, Beebe did not use these free photographs in his articles and books, most likely because he distrusted and disliked government—sentiments strongly expressed in his later writings. However, living in New York City, he had opportunities to see the government-sponsored work first hand. The Museum of Modern Art produced an exhibition, "Road to Victory," curated by Edward Steichen (then director of the Naval Aviation Photographic Unit) in 1942 with many FSA-OWI photographs.[7]

"Pictorial" photographers—who favored attractive backgrounds and skies—also were influential. J. Ghislain Lootens (1901–1946), who taught classes at the Brooklyn YMCA for ten years, was among the prominent pictorialists. *Lootens on Pho-*

Baltimore & Ohio, BC0102

Texas & Pacific, BC0992

Wadley Southern, BC0921

Colorado & Southern, BC0289

Ferdinand, BC0422

Frankfort & Cincinnati, BC2151

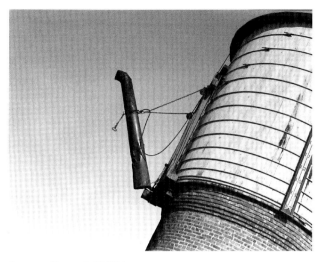
Raritan River, BC2550

Rio Grande Southern, BC3059

San Luis Valley Southern, BC1965

RGS no. 20 as Emma Sweeney, BC3308

Unadilla Valley, BC0674

Santa Fe, BC1010

tographic Enlarging and Print Quality (1944) featured samples of this style. He must have impressed Clegg, who studied with him and attributed his sense of balance and composition to Lootens.[8]

Although Beebe and Clegg commissioned a number of paintings, art never captured their imagination with the same passion as strong photography. "The photographs are many and magnificent. Dynamic and lyrical, they powerfully evoke the sights, sounds, and smells of railroading and what these mean to us; they put to shame the colored reproductions of six oil paintings which accompany them," Horace Reynolds wrote about *Mixed Train Daily* in 1947.[9]

Despite these influences, it is likely that Beebe and Clegg drew visual inspiration from their early family lives. Both families were participants in and patrons of the arts. Lucius' father and older brother were photographers. Clegg's mother was a fashion illustrator who possessed a wonderful eye.

Beebe's life as a drama critic in New York brought him into the world of the brilliant and fashionable creative leisure class. He frequented elite nightclubs and restaurants. (Jerome Zerbe, Beebe's companion in the 1930s, was the only celebrity photographer permitted inside El Morocco from 1934 to 1939.) In these circumstances, an intelligent figure like Beebe could not help but discern the abundant opportunities in photography. Zerbe also had friends at *Life,* who showcased his work in features such as "Zerbe Achieves Representative Portrait of New York Society."[10]

A specific influence, which shaped Beebe's long-lasting fascination with dramatic angled closeup views of the fronts of locomotives, came from Ivan Dmitri, who illustrated a 1936 Beebe article about luxury travel in *Town & Country*.[11] Dmitri was the pseudonym used by etching and watercolor artist Levon West (1900–1968) for his photography. His photos of trains often appeared in Beebe/Clegg books, such as Beebe's *High Iron,*[12] and "Ivan Dmitri Rides the Aristocrat" in *Age of Steam*.[13] Dmitri illustrated railroad articles in the *Saturday Evening Post,* including "Going, Going, Not Yet Gone" in 1942,[14] a feature about narrow-gauge lines. The feature could have inspired a chapter in *Mixed Train Daily,* as it lacked only Beebe's distinctive style of writing. Dmitri liked railroads as more than just a subject for his camera. In "L'Amour de Choo-Choo," the *Post* wrote that "we'd hardly bat an eye if we learned that he was living in a roundhouse on Park Avenue."[15]

Although Beebe, and later Clegg, had their own way of documenting railroading, their recognition of the importance of photography contributed to their successful entry into the book business.

These influences helped make *Mixed Train Daily* an unqualified triumph. More importantly, they added to the impact of a long series of books which expanded to feature the photography of others.

Notes

1. "Charlotte Division," *Life,* May 2, 1938.
2. David P, Morgan, "A Page Out of Life," *Trains,* April 1980, 40-41.
3. "They're Crowding the Rails," *Fortune,* June 1942.
4. "The Rock Island," *Life,* Feb. 25, 1946, 93-103.
5. "*Life* Rides a Milk Train in Vermont," *Life,* Aug. 17 1942, 13: 88-90, 92.
6. John Gruber, ed., *Railroaders: Jack Delano's Homefront Photography* (Madison, Wis.: Center for Railroad Photography & Art, 2014), 21.
7. "Road to Victory," *Bulletin of the Museum of Modern Art*, vol. 9, nos. 5-6, June 1942.
8. J. Ghislain Lootens, *Lootens on Photographic Enlarging and Print Quality* (Baltimore, Md.: The Camera, 1944).
9. Horace Reynolds, review of *Mixed Train Daily, New York Times,* Oct. 5, 1947, BR 14.
10. "Zerbe Achieves Representative Portrait of New York Society." *Life,* June 14, 1948, 46.
11. Lucius Beebe, "Keeping Up With the Casey Joneses," *Town & Country*, June 1936, 50-55, with photos by Ivan Dmitri. Thanks to Michael Zega for suggesting this reference.
12. Dmitri photos appear on pages 154, 156, and 205 of Beebe, *High Iron*.
13. "Ivan Dmitri Rides the Aristocrat" in Beebe and Clegg, *The Age of Steam* (New York, Toronto: Rinehart & Co. 1957), 270-271: see also page 51.
14. "Going, Going, Not Yet Gone," *Saturday Evening Post,* April 25, 1942, 20-21, 103, 105.
15. "L'Amour de Choo-Choo," in Keeping Posted, *Saturday Evening Post,* June 20, 1943, 4.

Live Oak, Perry & Gulf, BC2412

DeKalb & Western, BC0385

Denver & Rio Grande Western *Prospector*, BC1103

Illinois Central, BC1135

Midland Valley, BC3599

Reading, BC2584

3 The Visual Influences 51

Beebe and Clegg Boost Western Pacific's Image

Beebe and Clegg joined in grand celebrations at the Western Pacific. In addition to writing about the *California Zephyr* for *Holiday* (January 1950), they participated in at least two anniversaries. At Oakland's Third Street Station, they stand, talking with Gilbert H. Kneiss, assistant to WP's president, on March 3, 1953, the fiftieth anniversary of WP's incorporation (facing page). A parade of antique automobiles carried WP officials from San Francisco to a special train, pulled by historic WP steam locomotive no. 94. The special, with Beebe and Clegg's *Gold Coast* at the end of the train and reserved for a simulated Western Pacific directors meeting, pulled out of Oakland for Sacramento behind the *California Zephyr*. Kneiss (1899–1964) played a pivotal role in creating the public image of the WP in the late 1940s and early 1950s. He was a charter member of the Pacific Coast Chapter of the Railway & Locomotive Historical Society. In the photo above, Clegg poses with (from left) John M. Budd, president of the Great Northern, Frederic B. Whitman, president of the Western Pacific, and Beebe, at a November 10, 1951, ceremony honoring the twentieth anniversary of the Inland Gateway route linking the two railroads. Beebe and Clegg are in stylish morning suits. California State Railroad Museum, BCP0216 (facing page); Western Pacific, David P. Morgan Library, Kalmbach Publishing Co. (above).

4 Main Lines and Limiteds

Lucius Beebe had three railroad books under his belt when he joined forces with Charles Clegg. They produced the fourth book together, *Highball: A Pagent of Trains*. Beebe's consistent ability to attract well-known reviewers for the books demonstrated his knack for promotion, a trait important to later successes.

In the introduction to his first railroad picture-book, *High Iron: A Book of Trains* (1938), he described railroading as "the most heroic of American legends."[1] *High Iron* continued his association with Appleton-Century, which began with his *Boston and the Boston Legend* and ended with the fourth railroad book in 1945.

Beebe made no claims to *High Iron* being definitive, general railroad history. Rather, Beebe selected photographs "that have stirred the imagination of the author or pleased his fancy." While they did not ignore small railroads, these early books illustrated the majesty of main-line railroading and their heavy freight and fast passenger trains. Beebe depicted a number of diesel locomotives, a practice he shunned in later books. Steam was his clear favorite. He did not hide his dislike of diesel locomotives, a theme expressed in all his railroad books. "There is a wonder and a beauty of the *City of Los Angeles* but there is not motion and there is not the stirring thunder of exhaust," he wrote.[2]

Among many positive reviews was commentary from Rogers E. M. Whitaker (1899–1981), a *New Yorker* editor who also wrote under the pen name E. M. Frimbo. He said "*High Iron* represents the finest collation of railway action shots yet published. Many of the best pictures are the author's own handiwork." Whitaker noticed "some minor errata which escaped Mr. Beebe's eye," but concluded that "one has only to return to the pictures again to forget these few strictures."[3]

The "minor errata" and lavish praise were common themes in Whitaker's reviews of Beebe's books, but the books sold well.

Later, Beebe told Freeman Hubbard, editor of *Railroad* magazine, that *High Iron* was "a crude thing by sophisticated present day standards, but it seemed to touch off a lot of other railroad books."

While taking photographs for his second book in 1939 outside the Army's arsenal at Watertown, Massachusetts, Beebe attracted police attention. For the crime of pointing his camera at a passenger train pulled by locomotive no. 601 on the Boston & Albany's four-track main line, police suspected him of being a spy. The incident drew publicity due to Beebe's status as a writer for the *New York Herald Tribune*, including in a paragraph in *Newsweek*.[4]

"Speeding to the scene, the police found only Lucius Beebe, a New York Café Society columnist, taking a snapshot of a train with the arsenal as a background. Trains are Beebe's hobby," the weekly magazine said.[5] No more was said by the police, and a 2015 Freedom of Information request did not turn up any reference to Beebe in the FBI files.[6]

Beebe got more ink from gossip columnist Walter Winchell, who wrote in "On Broadway," "Lucius Beebe (almost arrested as a German spy near the Watertown Arsenal Satdee, while taking pictures of railroad tracks) writes: 'When I identified myself to the police chief, he said, 'Oh, this bird

Clegg, the pictorialist, captured a domineering plume of smoke rising vertically from Santa Fe locomotive 3214 and balanced the image with four crossbars of the railroad's pole line. The brakeman stands on the locomotive, indicating it is shoving up Raton Pass. The train is at Morley, Colorado, about 1945. The cone-shaped pile in the background is the slack pile from making coke. Clegg, California State Railroad Museum, BC1629

Policemen questioned Beebe for being a prospective German spy in 1939 after he photographed this Boston & Albany passenger train, pulled by locomotive 601, on the four-track main line at Allston outside the Army's arsenal at Watertown, Massachusetts. The arsenal is 500 feet to the left of Beebe, across the Charles River. The tower on the main building of the Perkins School for the Blind stands at the extreme right of the photo. Today this scene is the middle of the eight-lane Massachusetts Turnpike. A similar photo appears in the first issue of *Trains* and in *Age of Steam*, page 39. Beebe, California State Railroad Museum, BC1101

can't be no Natzi. He's all the time in Winchell's column.' So thanks, pal, Lucius."[7] [Winchell's spelling has been retained.]

Beebe provided further details when he later lamented the "widespread public delusion" that artists and photographers are viewed as spies. "Last year this department was surrounded by machine-gun-armed police while photographing trains at Allston, Massachusetts, and shrewdly questioned as to his intentions because, indeed, the Watertown Arsenal was located a mile and a half away, behind the contours of the New England skyline and across the expanse of the Charles River."[8]

In a letter to the editor of the *Herald Tribune*, written in his typical prose, Beebe commented, "The writer happens to be an amateur of railroad photography, and from the attentions his mainline safaris receive from the bumpkin constabulary and impertinent casuals one would imagine that every action shot of the *Broadway Limited* was the most prized objective of the Gestapo and the potential ruin of all Americas."[9]

Quickly moving on to his third book, *Highliners: A Railroad Album* (1940), Beebe praised the steam locomotive, presenting it in his first horizontal-format publication. "It has dominated the American imagination as it has the nation's economic destinies: as the ships of the world's oceans have laid hold upon the sensibilities of Englishmen since long before the time of Taliesin, the last great Druid."[10]

In *Highliners*, Beebe defined the perfect railroad action photograph; "With its rural background, its clarity of definition of all moving parts, its indication of speed through smoke and steam exhaust, its full length view of the entire train, and its absence of any object or matter to distract attention from the locomotive and consist themselves—is not easy to come by."[11]

Whitaker praised the photographs in the review he wrote for *Highliners*, calling them "excellent in various ways: some for their drama, some for sheer beauty of mechanical composition." He noted the lack of "rare museum pieces" on the Boston & Maine, Western Maryland, Erie, and Rutland, concluding Beebe could take these "as the nucleus for another command performance."[12]

In his review for the *Herald Tribune*, Whitaker called *Trains in Transition* the best of Beebe's photographic collections published so far. "To the uninitiate, many of them should appear simply for their pictorial quality, the lovely contrast of light and shadow, of motion against a pictorial background." He went on to defend Beebe's admiration of steam locomotives. "Whatever diesel locomotive or Greyhound bus or TWA sleeper plane roars in its wake, the plough that really broke the Western plain was the steam locomotive, and because of it this nation became a nation almost overnight."[13]

Beebe took a hiatus from photography during the war while Clegg served in the Navy. He wrote a non-railroad book, *Snoot If You Must* (1943), and reviewer Dorothy Parker concluded: "I see that Mr. Beebe's *Snoot If You Must* (it is surely some dark, dark masochism that makes me say that title again) is widely advertised for the Christmas trade. It must be what I believe is known as a gift book. That is to say, a book which you wouldn't take on any other terms."[14]

As World War II neared its end, Clegg and Beebe set off with cameras, traveling from coast to coast. They covered main lines and short lines and produced a vast array of images. Clegg's distinctive style of photography emerged in *Highball: A Pageant of Trains*, released late in 1945, with sixty of his photographs. It was his first book with Beebe. For the first time, a single train could be viewed from the individual perspective of each photographer, such as the scenes at Tunnel 1 on the Denver & Rio Grande Western (pages 82 and 83).

Beebe praised Clegg's contributions to the book, writing that "a study of his photographs in this book will reveal a devotion to the atmosphere and wonder of railroading not often encountered."[15]

Among others, Beebe acknowledged Jerry Arzrouni of Eastman Kodak Company of New York, who had apparently helped Beebe get film durng a period of wartime restrictions, which required "the most authoritative assistance."[16] Eastman Kodak displayed photos from the book in the windows of its New York store.[17]

For its review, the *Herald Tribune* turned to Stewart Holbrook, a nationally known journalist and historian from Oregon. He said that Beebe's earlier three books "made valuable contributions to the pictorial history of the rails, and the present work carries on the panorama." Holbrook praised the "well taken and chosen" photographs but did not mention Clegg's role in the book.[18]

In the *New York Times,* a reviewer identified only as N.K.B. called it "an entertaining and informative combination of effervescent, ambidextrous prose and spending prose." Beebe's four volumes "give a generous picture of American railroad history," he or she concluded.[19]

Beebe's introduction to *Highliners* provided a preview of their next and greatest project—the little railroads that had been living on borrowed time. "The end of the wars and the restoration of competition in the field of transportation, both of passengers and of merchandise, must inevitably spell the end of many short lines in the Deep South and Middle West," he wrote.[20] With the publication of *Mixed Train Daily*, their place in railroad book publishing was assured.

Beebe and Clegg aimed their cameras at a range of locomotives. Beebe shows Southern Pacific AC-9 no. 3804, an articulated locomotive, at Sparks, Nevada (above), and Clegg a Great Northern electric entering the Cascade Tunnel in Washington (facing page). California State Railroad Museum, BC3280, BC2291

Notes

1. Lucius Beebe, Introduction to *High Iron: A Book of Trains* (New York, London: D Appleton-Century Co., 1938), 3.

2. Beebe, *High Iron,* Introduction, 9.

3. Rogers E. M. Whitaker, "In Praise of Locomotives," review, *New York Herald Tribune,* Oct. 30, 1938.

4. The full story is in John Gruber, "A Spy? No, Just a Photographer," *Railroad History* 214, Spring-Summer 2016, 4-5.

5. "Dies and Spies," *Newsweek,* Oct. 16, 1939, 34.

6. Gruber, FBI, Freedom of Information Act request, June 18, 2015, personal files.

7. Walter Winchell, "On Broadway," from *Burlington (N.C.) Daily Times,* Oct. 20, 1939.

8. Beebe, "This New York," *Herald Tribune,* Dec. 28, 1940, 16.

9. Beebe, "Not All Are Spies," *Herald Tribune,* April 4, 1941, 22.

10. Beebe, Foreword, *Highliners: A Railroad Album* (New York, London: D Appleton-Century Co., 1940), vii.

11. Beebe, Introduction, *Highliners,* ix.

12. Whitaker, "Choo-Choo, Choo-Choo!," review, *Herald Tribune,* April 7, 1940.

13. Whitaker, "Toward Streamliners," review, *Herald Tribune,* Dec. 7, 1941, H6.

14. Dorothy Parker, *Saturday Review of Literature,* Dec. 11, 1943.

15. Beebe, Introduction, *Highball: A Pageant of Trains* (New York, London: D. Appleton-Century Co., 1945), 8.

16. Beebe, Introduction, *Highball,* 9.

17. Book Notes, *Herald Tribune,* Jan. 17, 1946.

18. Steward Holbrook, "Railway Glories, Smokestack to Caboose," review, *Herald Tribune,* Dec. 23, 1945, E5.

19. N.K.B., "Balling the Jack With Beebe," *New York Times,* review, Jan. 13, 1946, BR11.

20. Beebe, Introduction, *Highball,* 6.

Early lightweight trains in the Midwest attracted Beebe's attention. The first diesel-powered streamliner, the *Pioneer Zephyr,* is shown departing Kansas City Union Station for its round trip to Omaha and Lincoln (facing page, top, *Highliners,* picture 64). The popularity of the service required the Burlington to add a car. The original, three-car train is preserved in Chicago's Museum of Science and Industry. St. Louis Union Station was also busy with the new trainsets. Alton's *Abraham Lincoln* (facing page, bottom) and Illinois Central's *Green Diamond* (above) competed on the Chicago–St. Louis run. The *Zephyr* and *Green Diamond* passenger cars are articulated for weight savings. Beebe, three photos, California State Railroad Museum, BC0900, BC0080, BC2459

4 Main Lines and Limiteds

A portfolio of streamlined steam locomotives shows the creative work of industrial designers. Above, a Grand Trunk Western passenger train led by 4-8-4 no. 6407 storms across northern Indiana. In the Chicago area, Chicago & North Western and Milwaukee Road were strong competitors yet purchased 4-6-4 locomotives built to the same specifications. C&NW's *Overland Limited* backs into the Chicago Passenger Terminal (facing page, above, *High Iron*, page 110). Milwaukee's fast-running *Hiawatha* speeds along near Lake Forest, Illinois (facing page, below, *Trains in Transition*, page 171). Beebe, three photos, California State Railroad Museum, BC1180, BC0219, BC1064

4 Main Lines and Limiteds 63

Reading's *Crusader*, a Jersey City-to-Philadelphia train, is "hitting it up" on the main line on a winter morning just outside the Jersey City Terminal Yards (Beebe, above, *Highliners,* picture 36). California State Railroad Museum, BC2524

New York Central's *Mercury* approaches Englewood station in Chicago (facing page, above); its locomotive, the *Commodore Vanderbilt*, was the first streamlined steam locomotive. New Haven's streamlined "Shoreliner" class locomotive steams out of the Boston yard with the *Gilt Edge Limited* (facing page, below, *High Iron,* page 78). Beebe, California State Railroad Museum, BC2646, BC1150

4 Main Lines and Limiteds 65

A Boston & Maine special train with wooden commuter coaches rounds a curve headed for the Rockingham Park racetrack at Salem, New Hampshire. Beebe, California State Railroad Museum, BC0131

Delaware & Hudson's *Laurentian* travels along the main tracks (facing page, top, Clegg, *Hear the Train Blow,* page 362). Beebe's unusual going-away view shows an Erie Railroad caboose and tank cars, framed with the pole line. California State Railroad Museum, BC0391, BC2206

4 Main Lines and Limiteds 67

A sample of eastern railroading: A Jersey Central camelback steams under an impressive signal bridge (Beebe, facing page, above). A Pennsy freight train "clattering down" the electrified main line near Princeton Junction, New Jersey (Beebe, facing page, below, *Trains in Transition,* page 54). Just south of the Delaware Water Gap, a Lehigh & New England train leaves New Jersey and crosses the Delaware River into Pennsylvania. It is westbound to Pen Argyle which was L&NE's main shops and yard. At the near end of the bridge (PA side) is the DL&W's "Old Road" line; note lineside telegraph pole below (Clegg, above). California State Railroad Museum, BC0146, BC2276, BC2294

This Delaware, Lackawanna & Western train is eastbound on the Paulinskill Viaduct in Hainesburg, New Jersey. The Delaware Water Gap is in the distance. The slightly darker arch illustrates where the NYS&W crossed underneath. The morning light suggests the train is the *Merchants Express* bringing shoppers from Scranton to New York City with its usual 4-6-2 in charge (Clegg, top). California State Railroad Museum, BC1497

Beebe objected to the "untidy and unbuttoned appearance" of the missing front coupler shroud on this Pennsy train, shown approaching 47th Street in Chicago. Pennsy line here is four tracks wide, while the Chicago & Western Indiana is at far left as it begins to curve into its station at 47th Street. C&WI's 40th Street Tower is visible by the truss bridge in the distance. The truss bridge carried the "L" line to the Stock Yards on air rights constructed above the Chicago Junction Railway (Clegg, *Highball*, page 123). California State Railroad Museum, BC2268

Beebe titled it "On the Outside Iron" but provided no details about this steam freight train on the Pennsylvania Railroad's electrified main line in Maryland (Beebe, *High Iron,* page 141). California State Railroad Museum, BC3528

Beebe enjoyed depicting the heroic image of mighty power pulling heavy tonnage, passenger or freight. Chesapeake & Ohio no. 546, a 4-8-2 built by Baldwin in 1919, is unmistakably C&O with the front-mounted air brake pumps and low headlight. This photograph appears in *When Beauty Rode the Rails* on p. 185 and in Al Staufer's 1965 *C&O Power*. California State Railroad Museum, BC0174

Beebe with camera appears in the left corner of Clegg's photograph of a Southern Railway stock train, with locomotive no. 691, on the Southern main line in northern Virginia, about 1945 (facing page, above). Beebe's photo at the same location is in *Highball,* page 67. Beebe watches as a Richmond, Fredericksburg & Potomac train passes an industrial site in Virginia (Clegg, facing page, below). Typically, if Beebe appeared in a photo he was cropped off or as here, the photo was not printed in a book. California State Railroad Museum, BC2023, BC2617

4 Main Lines and Limiteds 73

A typical Cincinnati, New Orleans & Texas Pacific Ms-4-class Mikado with Wimble smoke duct over boiler is southbound less than a mile south of Oneida, Tennessee (Beebe, above). Louisville & Nashville trains pass a coaling tower at Paris, Kentucky (Clegg, facing page, above) and cross a river and start running on a street in an unidentified city (Clegg, facing page, below). California State Railroad Museum, BC2019, BC2676, BC2677

4 Main Lines and Limiteds 75

A Rock Island *Rocket* (Beebe, facing page, above) is at Tower 55 on the east side of Fort Worth, Texas, crossing the Texas & Pacific. Missouri-Kansas-Texas workers often made inspection trips in an automobile fitted with flanged wheels and a self-contained turntable. Here, about 1945, the automobile is being removed from the tracks at Staley Tower in Oklahoma, three miles north of Denison, Texas (Clegg, facing page, below). The photo of a short Missouri-Kansas-Texas passenger train lacks the smoke so prized by the photographers (above). California State Railroad Museum, BC1523, BC2885, BC2884

A St. Louis-San Francisco (Frisco) freight train rounds a curve on the railway's single-track main line. The white streaks are caused by defective film development (Beebe, above). Colorado & Southern passenger train (Beebe, right) climbs a short grade at Holloway, Colorado, on its way to Denver (A similar photo appears on page 192 of *Highball*). In a dramatic vertical photo from 1946, a Kansas City Southern freight shows mostly steam coming from its stack—a contrast to the black smoke preferred by photographers (Clegg, facing page). California State Railroad Museum, BC1851, BC0249, BC1381

The Denver & Rio Grande Western was a favorite Beebe-Clegg mountain railroad. West of Denver, a double-headed passenger train climbs toward Tunnel 1 in an unusual, creative photo (Clegg, facing page, above). A double-headed stock extra moves east out of Alamosa at Blanca toward LaVeta Pass (Clegg, facing page, below, *MTD,* page 175, *Rio Grande,* page 69). Beebe describes "an amazing series of convolutions" as the first section of Rio Grande's *Exposition Flyer* gains altitude between Leyden, Colorado, and Tunnel 1 (Beebe, above, *Highball,* page 189). California State Railroad Museum, BC3791, BC1899, BC1120

Two photographers, two perspectives, same train. D&RGW diesel freight from the top of Tunnel 1 outside Denver has Clegg's eye for framing with trees. D&RGW 546 was an EMD FT built in December 1943 and delivered as a four-unit set, 546A-546B-546C-546D (facing page). Beebe photographed the same train from trackside at the bottom of a nearby cut (above, *Highball,* page 187). California State Railroad Museum, BC1883, BC1122

On the facing page, Union Pacific trains pick up train orders at Borie, Wyoming, a junction eleven miles west of Cheyenne where the Denver line joins the main line (page 193, *Age of Steam*). Above, Union Pacific's *Overland Limited*, a Chicago to Oakland train, storms past Tower A on its way west from Cheyenne. The view dates to some time after 1954 due to the presence of new signal equipment. Beebe, three photos, California State Railroad Museum, BC0850, BC0810, BC0825

A magnificent Daylight locomotive, no. 4448, heads up Southern Pacific train 72, as indicated on the side of the locomotive, the all-stops mail and express train from San Francisco to Los Angeles (above). Beebe misidentified the train as a northbound and the location as Oxnard on page 399 of *The Central Pacific and the Southern Pacific Railroads*, an impossibility since the train number tells us the train is headed to Los Angeles. According to a 1943 timetable, train 72 departed Oxnard at 4:12 a.m.; it is more likely that the train is shown somewhere in the Bay Area. Beebe, California State Railroad Museum, BC3301

An eastbound Union Pacific freight train sends a dramatic plume of smoke skyward as it approaches lower quadrant automatic block signal 563.6. Below the number plate, the signal has a round yellow plate with a "P" on it, indicating that this was a "permissive" signal. The overpass in the background is U.S. highway 287, which crosses the UP just east of Laramie, Wyoming. Beebe, California State Railroad Museum, BC0854

In "Symbols of Integrated Power" Beebe shows the valve gear and part of the rod assembly of one of Santa Fe's 3765 series, 4-8-4 high-speed passenger locomotives. Beebe, *Highliners,* picture 94. California State Railroad Museum, BC1019

The heavy grades of Raton Pass on the Colorado-New Mexico border always challenged the Santa Fe. Here, a westbound double-headed passenger train climbs the pass south of Starkville, Colorado. Clegg, California State Railroad Museum, BC1585

Clegg titled the above photo, "The Santa Fe *Chief*, Double Heading in the Raton" (*Highball*, page 190). At right, an articulated locomotive accelerates in the morning with the north side of Raton, New Mexico, in the background; the view is looking due east. Clegg, two photos, California State Railroad Museum, BC1623, BC1619

Southern Pacific passenger trains covered a wide geographic area. Passengers stand on the platform, ready to board the *City of San Francisco* at Berkeley, California, as the train heads for Chicago. The station stands today; the location is an Amtrak stop (above). Beebe, David P. Morgan Library, Kalmbach Publishing Company

A cab-forward rounds a curve with the Sunday-only Sparks, Nevada-to-Oakland local just west of Truckee, California (facing page, above; the photo appears in the preview and premier issues of *Trains* and *Age of Steam* (page 158). Beebe, David P. Morgan Library, Kalmbach Publishing Company

The view of the *Sunset Limited,* train no. 1 (facing page, below), shows the westbound train on Beaumont Hill at Garnet, California, a helper station in steam days. Beebe, California State Railroad Museum, BC1827

4 Main Lines and Limiteds 93

Cajon Pass near San Bernardino, California, is a spectacular photo location. Union Pacific's *Pacific Limited* negotiates tight curves in 1946 (Clegg, above). This curve was also extensively photographed by Herbert Sullivan for whom the location is named. A Santa Fe diesel with white flags moves a heavy freight train through the pass (Beebe, right). California State Railroad Museum, BC0841, BC1637

Southern Pacific freight train extra 5042, with a rear helper locomotive to attack California's Beaumont Hill, has "great sky great smoke," as noted on the back of the proof print. Beebe, California State Railroad Museum, BC3274

A Belated Salute to Casey Jones

After discovering that only an unpainted wooden cross stood at the grave of Casey (John Luther) Jones, Clegg and Beebe paid for a bronze and granite marker and dedicated the memorial to "perpetuate the legend of American railroading and the man who became the symbol of daring and romance." Attending the ceremony on August 7, 1947, at Mt. Calvary Cemetery in Jackson, Mississippi, are, from left: Charles Jones, Casey's son; Barbara Jones, his fourteen-year-old granddaughter, who unveiled the marker; Clegg; Simm Webb, Casey's fireman; Mrs. Jane Brady Jones, Casey's widow; Mayor George Smith of Jackson; and Beebe. On the facing page, Beebe, Clegg, and Mrs. Jones stand next to the marker. Casey died at the throttle in Vaughan, Mississippi, in 1900 while trying to make up time with a late passenger train, an event celebrated in a well-known folk song. California State Railroad Museum, BCP0867, BCP0866

4 Main Lines and Limiteds 97

Propelled by an awareness that the world was on the cusp of major changes, Beebe and Clegg devoted their postwar efforts to chasing the last vestiges of small-scale shortline railroading. The antithesis of big trains and fast limiteds of mainline railroads, these shortlines toiled in isolation that was rapidly being penetrated by networks of highways and truck transportation. Extinction loomed.

Beebe and Clegg spent three years preparing *Mixed Train Daily*. The railroads they documented had distinct and individual personalities yet shared many common traits. They were where every journey started and ended, where the coming of the train was a social event at the depot. They were community lifelines, where the little train went out to meet the big train and touched the commerce of the nation. They were rolling museums, where aged steam locomotives towed swaying cars down weedy tracks. They were everything that spoke to a simpler, slower, more intimate time, and they were a fraying thread in the American experience.

Beebe's interview with a *Washington Post* society columnist provided insight into their reasons for doing the book, which he and Clegg started working on in 1944. He explained their motives: "The most obvious and simplest of these was that the short line, as a microcosm of the whole pageant of railroading, was fast disappearing and that

5 Short Lines: "Not as Long but Just as Wide"

its flavor of individualism, its wonderful archaisms and absolescences of operations, motive power, and rolling stock would soon be a legend," he told Mary Van Rensselaer Thayer.[1] Thayer was a well-known journalist in the U.S. and abroad who later wrote two books about Jacqueline Kennedy Onassis.[2]

Beebe continued to tell about the book and short lines. "Their functions, their operations, and their physical properties, no less than the outland serenities of their existence, were a complete negation of monolithic industrialism, a brief and wistful souvenir of yesterday in a civilization which embraced the income tax, the elm blight, woman suffrage, game wardens, the assembly line, the atom

In "The Coaches of Yesterday," Beebe writes about the combine (combination baggage car-coach) of Georgia's Wrightsville & Tennille with a compartment dividing its white and colored sections. Neither Beebe (at right) nor their automobile (behind him) appeared in the published picture (Clegg, MTD, page 279). California State Railroad Museum, BC0887

bomb, and the Roosevelt family."

Mrs. Thayer knew his habits and how to find him. The conversation, conducted by telephone from the Biltmore's Turkish baths in New York City, proved to be one of the rare times when Beebe provided commentary on their cross-country travels rather than the usual promotional message.

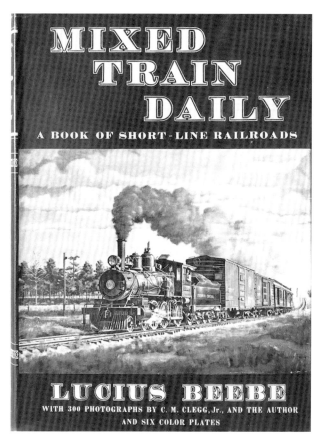

The dust jacket of *Mixed Train Daily* features a painting by Howard Fogg, not a photograph. Joe McMillan collection

"We discovered that the dollar steak dinner still exists in Waynesboro, Georgia, and Corinth, Mississippi; that the ultimate in hospitality in Jackson, Tennessee, was an offer of 'unstamped' whiskey, distilled, thank God, in complete defiance of the Federal Government; that in the Far West no motorist would pass a stalled stranger without an offer of assistance, and that in Nevada, the fairest Commonwealth in the Star-Spangled Union, there are no taxes at all and that the roulette wheel and faro bank pay for all public good works. In a word, we discovered that all America is not neatly regimented along U.S. no. 1 or outside the club car windows of the *City of Los Angeles*," Beebe said. In Kentucky, they were guests of Henry Wadsworth of Maysville.[3]

Beebe and Clegg started their research for *Mixed Train Daily* in 1944, drawing their initial inspiration from the paintings of Sheldon Pennoyer and such publications as the Railway & Locomotive Historical Society Bulletin.[4] Beebe and Clegg were not the first to publish about shortline railroading, but they were the first to marry engaging prose with lavish illustration.

Beebe reviewed Archie Robertson's *Slow Train to Yesterday*, about "the vanishing local train," for the *Herald Tribune*. Robertson published his book in 1945[5]—a full year after Beebe and Clegg began work on *Mixed Train Daily*. Beebe's review displayed a working knowledge of these small railroads and hinted coyly at a forthcoming Beebe-Clegg book, writing that "the field can stand a great deal more exploitation."

Andrew Merrilees, a Canadian railroad collector and contemporary of Beebe, told Louis Saillard[6] that Robertson influenced the direction of Beebe's work. Beebe acknowledged in *Mixed Train Daily* that Robertson had been to places before him, and said, "In a sense, the authors were able to find pay dirt only because Robertson had no camera."[7]

Beebe recorded the segregated "Jim Crow" cars of the mixed freight and passenger trains in the South, whose cars had baggage doors in their center with separate "colored" and "white" sections on each side. While the cars were typical in the South of Beebe's time, these photographs have become rare and significant contributions to the historical record, providing a window into a world of prejudice against minority populations. Ironically, Beebe and Clegg's wealth and status insulated them from discrimination they otherwise would have faced as a gay couple in the 1940s and 1950s.

Not all the locations were friendly. Beebe noted that especially in rural areas, such as Winnfield, Louisiana, strangers with cameras were viewed with suspicion. "The authors have been assured by no less a super sleuth than J. Edgar Hoover that his mail is considerably augmented by well-meaning informants whenever they have ventured forth in search of railroad photographs."[8]

Their biggest triumph and the best of their promotional efforts was, "*Life* Goes to a Party," which

Beebe's quiet, pastoral going-away view of the nine-mile long Sandersville Railroad in Georgia serves as an introductory photo for *Mixed Train Daily* (top, *MTD*, page v). The railroad connects Kaolin and Tennille. Both photos show the unpaved roads of the rural South of the era (above). Beebe, California State Railroad Museum, BC1757, BC1751

5 Short Lines: "Not as Long but Just as Wide" 101

brought national coverage of *Mixed Train Daily* via the country's leading pictorial weekly.[9] Beebe sponsored a rolling party on Sunday, September 14, 1947, traveling over the Maryland & Pennsylvania from Baltimore to Delta to introduce the new book.[10] *Life* wrote that "guests tried to recapture the bone-rattling atmosphere of a bygone era."

The formal book introduction came the next day, September 15, 1947, when publisher E.P. Dutton & Co. invited reporters and editors to meet the authors at a cocktail party at the Hotel St. Regis in New York.[11]

Mixed Train Daily was an immediate success. Beebe sent a telegram to Clegg, saying "you are best seller in Sunday's *Times*." It ranked thirteenth in a list of general books—an amazing feat for a railroad book.[12] It was third in nonfiction in Chicago and listed among the best-selling books in Denver.

Beebe acknowledged Clegg's role in an autographed copy, writing across the endpapers, "For Chuck, who had the idea, did the work, and made the book, in gratitude and affection."[13]

An unexpected source for promotion came from company publications of the main-line railroads. The *Milwaukee Road Magazine* called Beebe the country's leading authority on short-line railroads, and continued with a sentence only Beebe himself could have written: "And, indeed, Mr. Beebe is equally at ease in the habiliment of the drawing room and the wide-brimmed Stetson clomping boots he wears on his rugged safaris down the by-paths of the main line." The magazine included photos of connecting short lines such as the Copper Range in Upper Michigan and the Manchester & Oneida in Iowa, plus a view of the dedication of a memorial headstone for Casey Jones in Tennessee.[14] Other company magazines mentioning *Mixed Train Daily* included *Erie Railroad Magazine*, October 1947; *Tracks, GM&O News*, August 15, 1947; *Atlantic Coast Line News*, August 1947; *Northwestern Newsliner*, August 1947; *Texas & Pacific Topics*, August 1947; and *Western Pacific Headlight*, August 1947.[16]

Most reviewers were laudatory. Richard Overton, a Northwestern University professor, business historian, and founder of the Lexington Group in Transportation History, was not. In the *Chicago Sun*, he wrote that "anyone who cherishes in the slightest degree the elementary rules of good writing and the chastity of the English language should avoid this beguiling volume on pain of apoplexy. No pleas of the necessity of 'color' or 'atmosphere' can justify the self-conscious, obscure and altogether silly verbal contortions of the text." In his conclusion, he advised that if you share Beebe's "enthusiastic reverence" for short lines, "this is your book."[15]

Sterling North, an American writer best known for the children's book *Rascal*, wrote a review in verse "of a glamorous and nostalgic book" for the *Richmond Times Dispatch* that ended with a chorus:

The Lucius Beebe Special
(With old nostalgic hex}
And photos by Clegg, Jr.
The finest thing since sex.

A Colorado & South Eastern train moves slowly through a western landscape near Trinidad, Colorado (facing page). The massive smoke plume suggests that the photographer requested the fireman "turn on the smoke." If the fuel is burning well, there should not be a lot of smoke. The landscape is full of railroad and pictorial interest, hallmarks of Clegg's work. Rustic rail telegraph poles appear on the right. Fences, cattle, and another set of poles appear on the left. The fireman stands atop the tender. In the above photo, the train slowly clatters across a main line crossing. Clegg, two photos. California State Railroad Museum, BC3789, BC0287

Their photography found praise in New York City. Malcolm Cowley, writing in the *Herald Tribune,* liked Clegg's honest photographs. "There are hundreds of them, handsomely reproduced, and they make us almost hear the engine whistle at lonely crossings." But he noted that Beebe's text was not consistent with the short lines' "homely and day-to-day poetry. This is something that his style, which is neither homely nor poetic, doesn't always permit him to express. Still, he does manage to say that the short lines belong each to its own countryside, as the big roads never do."[17]

New York Times reviewer Horace Reynolds also liked the photographs, writing, "Dynamic and lyrical, they powerfully evoke the sights, sounds, and smells of railroading and what they mean to us; they put to shame the colored reproductions of six oil paintings which accompany them." Of Beebe's text, Reynolds said, "At his best, when he is truly moved, he puts aside his 'columnese' and writes with insight and grace."[18]

The railroad press recognized both authors' work. "It is unique, and I used the word advisedly. In all railroading there is nothing else like it. Until the Guggenheim Foundation or some other endowment fund sees fit to subsidize a gifted writer and photographer to ride a couple hundred short lines—and this is unlikely—Beebe and Clegg fear no competition," Frank P. Donovan Jr. wrote in *Trains.*[19]

While *Trains* devoted two pages to *Mixed Train Daily,* it reserved four for Robert W. Richardson article's "The Unreliable Mixed Train," which covered mixed trains on shortline and main-line railroads—an indication of the enduring interest in the topic. Richardson later helped found the Colorado Railroad Museum.

Railroad magazine praised Beebe and Clegg's photography by saying that the short lines "take life in their sensitive photographic portraits." The views are "unspoken history and will remain timeless," the reviewer, E. K., wrote. "*Mixed Train Daily* is the best proof that Beebe's shortline safari only increased his contempt for the 'monstrosities of diesel and the improbable turbine,'" E. K. also observed.[20]

Model Builder, published by the Lionel Corporation, promoted the book with a cover photo and feature story by Beebe about the Louisville & Wadley and Wadley Southern, two Georgia lines described as "superlatively satisfactory examples of short line railroading as it is still maintained and flourishes in the Deep South as of the year of 1947."[21]

In a 1956 issue of *Trains,* editor David P. Morgan listed *Mixed Train Daily* in a retrospective of the ten best railroad books and said that "Beebe's writing is its strength and durability."[22]

While the authors made almost all of the photographs, a few were taken by others such as Horace "Mike" D. Runey (*MTD* page 240) and Robert W. Richardson (*MTD* page 58). Runey soon gained recognition as a photographer of short lines, and Richardson for his devotion to Colorado narrow-gauge lines. It was also an indication of the future direction of Beebe and Clegg's books—an increasing emphasis on work by other photographers.

Not surprisingly, *Mixed Train Daily* had an impact on museums and railroad preservation. Prior to Beebe and Clegg, photography related primarily to main-line railroads. "Beebe and Clegg brought forth the concept of the rural railroad, opened a lot of eyes in this regard. It was an impressive effort. It had a bigger influence on local museums than on national museums. Short lines are local history personified," according to Ray Buhrmaster, an early member of Mid-Continent Railway Historical Society, North Freedom, Wisconsin. *Mixed Train Daily* provided ideas for planning the museum's short-line orientation, he added.[23]

In their photography and text, Beebe and Clegg focused on several railroads that would later be significant in the preservation world, including the East Broad Top and the Colorado narrow-gauge lines, all of which are recognized today as National Historic Landmarks.

Mixed Train Daily stands as Beebe and Clegg's most influential book, and its themes established the foundation for the next two decades of their writing.

Beebe described the Tremont & Gulf, which operated out of Winnfield, Louisiana, as "by far the most enterprising and functionally animate of short lines we encountered in the Deep South." A hog scurries off the tracks as the train stops for water at Grandstaff, Louisiana. Clegg, California State Railroad Museum, BC0621

Notes

1. Mary Van Rensselaer Thayer, "Lucius Found Dollar Steaks Amid Cinders," *Washington Post,* Oct. 14, 1947, B5.

2. J. Y. Smith, "Mary V. R. Thayer, Ex-Society Columnist, Dies," *Washington Post,* Dec. 14, 1983, B11.

3. *Louisville Courier-Journal,* Sept. 7, 1947.

4. Beebe, "About Little Railroads," *Herald Tribune,* Aug. 26, 1945, E2.

5. Archie Robertson, *Slow Train to Yesterday: A Last Glance at the Local* (Boston: Houghton Mifflin Co., 1945) and Tony Reevy, "Writers of the Rail: Elegy for Archie," *Railroad History* 187 (Fall-Winter 2002), 109-115.

6. Loius Saillard to John Gruber, May 9, 2016.

7. Lucius Beebe, Tremont & Gulf, in *Mixed Train Daily* (New York: E. P. Dutton & Co., 1947), 51.

8. Lucius Beebe, Tremont & Gulf, 98.

9. "Life Goes to a Party," *Life,* Oct. 13, 1947.

10. "Ma and Pa Line Runs Lucius Beebe Special," Hanover (Pa.) *Evening Sun,* Sept. 15, 1947.

11. Formal invitation, E. P. Dutton & Co. Holloway collection.

12. Keith L. Justice, *Bestseller Index: All Books, by Author, on the Lists of Publishers Weekly and the New York Times through 1990* (Jefferson, N.C.: McFarland & Co., 1998), 36.

13. Beebe to Clegg, autographed in *Mixed Train Daily,* Sept. 15, 1947. Holloway Collection.

14. "Lucius Beebe Immortalizes the Short Line," *Milwaukee Road Magazine* 35:6 (September 1947), 16-17.

15. Scrapbooks, E. P. Dutton & Co. records, Syracuse University Libraries.

16. Richard Overton, "'Mixed Train Daily' Into the American Past," *Chicago Sun,* Sept. 25, 1947.

17. Malcolm Cowley, "Books and Things," review, *Herald Tribune,* Sept. 16, 1947, 19.

18. Horace Reynolds, "Short-Line Railroads," review, *New York Times,* Oct. 5, 1947, BR 14.

19. Frank P. Donovan Jr., "The American Scene in Railroading," review, *Trains,* Nov. 1947, 59.

20. E.K. (E. M. Kennedy, associate editor), in "New Books," review, *Railroad,* Dec. 1947, 119-120.

21. Lucius Beebe, "Mixed Train Daily," *Model Builder,* September 1947.

22. Morgan, "Ten Best Books? ... One Man's Choice," *Trains,* Dec. 1956, 58.

23. Ray Buhrmaster, interview with John Gruber, Downers Grove, Ill., Nov. 17, 2016.

Passengers leave each end of the segregated Jim Crow car as workers unload mail and express from the middle section for exchange with another mixed train of the Georgia & Florida at Swainsboro, Georgia (above, *MTD*, page 32). On the Wadley Southern, one of the classic shortlines of the Old South, Beebe rides the rear platform of the combine as the northbound mixed travels from Wadley, Georgia, to Swainsboro (facing page, above). When the track is clear, workers wash down the platform of the Central of Georgia station at Wadley, used also by the Louisville & Wadley and Wadley Southern (facing page, below). The Wrightsville & Tennille, Louisville & Wadley, Wadley Southern, and Sylvania Central were subsidiaries of the Central of Geogia with common management and maintenance facilities at Dublin, Georgia. Equipment was used interchangeably among the four roads. Clegg, California State Railroad Museum, BC0883, BC0914, BC0919

The Marianna & Blountstown had its shops and yard at Blountstown, Florida. It was owed by Alfred F. Du Pont of Wilmington, Delaware (Clegg, left, *MTD*, page 15). Its afternoon train charges down the track with thunder clouds in the background (Beebe, below, *MTD*, page 14). California State Railroad Museum, BC2255, BC2256

Although its officials were suspicious of strangers with cameras, Clegg produced this view of Tremont & Gulf's morning eastbound mixed with locomotive no. 20 as it crosses the swamp trestle east of Rochelle, Louisiana (facing page, *MTD*, page 100). California State Railroad Museum, BC0612

Midland Valley no. 93, carrying a tender tank, rolls a short cut of freight cars eastward at Carpenter's Bluff, Texas (Clegg, above, *Highball,* page ii). On the Columbus & Greenville, a much-smaller motor car stops at Stewart, Mississippi (Clegg, right). California State Railroad Museum, BC2518, BC0333

A steam locomotive serves the Weatherford, Mineral Wells & Northwestern in east Texas, "a railroad with rich relatives." Beebe, California State Railroad Museum, BC0689

A study in contrasts; a modern diesel passenger train of the Gulf, Mobile & Ohio stops at Vinegar Bend, Alabama, which is also served by the woodburning trains of the Mississippi & Alabama Railroad (Clegg, facing page, above, photo appears in *Trains,* November 1946, and in Louis Saillard's article in the GM&OHS *News* No. 127, 2011). Beebe labeled the photo above, "The Last Wood-Burner of Them All" (Clegg, *MTD,* page 19, *Age of Steam,* page 106). California State Railroad Museum BC2346, BC2335

Clegg and Beebe found traces of wood burners all around them in Alabama and Louisiana. In the yards at Long Leaf, Louisiana, where the Crowell-Spencer Lumber Company railroad connected to the Missouri Pacific, discarded cabbage stacks wait to be scrapped. An overturned, rumpled steel boxcar lurks in the background (Clegg, facing page, below). California State Railroad Museum, BC2579

The Atlantic & Western Railway in North Carolina ran between Sanford and Lillington until 1961, when all but three miles from Sanford to Jonesboro were abandoned. Its steam train runs next to rows of corn (right) and stops at Broadway, a station on the now-abandoned section (below). Today, with added miles, it is part of Genesee & Wyoming. Clegg, two photos, California State Railroad Museum, BC1352, BC1349

A shop scene (top) on the Buffalo Creek & Gauley, a line that ran steam freight trains in West Virginia until 1965, shows work on BC&G 2-8-0 no. 5. It was built in 1904 by Alco-Richmond as Chesapeake & Ohio 509, class G-7, renumbered C&O 838 about 1926, and sold to the BC&G in 1933. It is believed to have been scrapped in 1953. Clegg, California State Railroad Museum, BC1505

In a scene repeated frequently in Georgia, merchandise is unloaded from a modern streamlined car, here from Central of Georgia's no. 1 (above), and reloaded into an ancient wood car, in this case a Sylvania Central combination car at Rocky Ford (facing page, below) in March 1946 views from *Mixed Train Daily* (page 38). A woman watches her crate of iced fish being unloaded for shipment to Sylvania. The railroad got the perishables to Sylvania in record time (facing page, above). "In the Sylvania Central may be seen vestigial traces of all the little railroads that came into being in the South at the conclusion of the 'Yankee War,'" Beebe wrote. Clegg, three photos, California State Railroad Museum, BC1798, BC1787, BC1788

The Smoky Mountain Railroad's mixed train "re-creates the simplicities of yesterday's railroading" as it moves along between Knoxville and Sevierville, Tennessee (above, *MTD,* page 81). "Its homely operations and country setting make it the very style and archetype of the more than 500 independently owned or operated short-line railroads in the United States," Beebe wrote at the beginning of *Mixed Train Daily.* Clegg, California State Railroad Museum, BC2007

Although a profitable railroad, the Georgia Northern showed all the characteristics of a rural, backwoods line, with cattle roaming across its tracks (top) and well-worn rail in its yards (above). Clegg, two photos, California State Railroad Museum, BC2727, BC2731

Gainesville Midland, with shops and yards in Gainesville, Georgia, was known for its fast-running Decapod locomotives. Its outdoor servicing facilities at Belmont were primitive, where an employee traverses a plank with a bucket-load of sand (above, Beebe, *Age of Steam,* page 110). Locomotives stand outside at Gainesville (facing page, above), where workers make repairs (facing page, below). Beebe, three photos, California State Railroad Museum, BC3562, BC3766, BC3707

5 Short Lines: "Not as Long but Just as Wide" 121

Beebe wrote eloquently about the Prescott & Northwestern, a rural Arkansas line, calling it one of the "most pastorally beautiful railroads in the land." Its once-a-week steam mixed train in June 1946 approaches the cattle guards of a highway crossing as two children from their nearby cabin watch its progress (Clegg, *MTD,* page 234). California State Railroad Museum, BC2574

The Tallulah Falls Railway operates northbound across "Big Cannon" or "Big Wiley" trestle in Wiley, Georgia, in June 1946 (facing page, top). In western Georgia, the Bowden Railway's sole piece of rolling stock, its motor car, serves a general store in Bowden (facing page, bottom, *MTD,* page 49). Clegg, two photos, California State Railroad Museum, BC1277, BC1048

124 Beebe & Clegg: Their Enduring Photographic Legacy

The St. Johnsbury & Lake Champlain stretches for ninety-six miles across "lushly tranquil" rural Vermont, in a land of covered bridges (Beebe, facing page, above) and heavy grades (Clegg, above). Its train stands in St. Johnsbury at a station shared with the Maine Central and Canadian Pacific (Clegg, facing page, below). California State Railroad Museum, BC3467, BC3473, BC3184

The daily mixed train of the Bellefonte Central rounds a curve on its westbound run between Bellefonte and State College, Pennsylvania (Beebe, right, *Highball,* page 29). At the Unadilla Valley's New Berlin yards in western New York, Clegg captured a view of workers performing a move known as a "flying switch" in September 1945 (below, *MTD,* page 249). California State Railroad Museum, BC1475, BC0653

Near the summit of Bergen Hill on the outskirts of South Amboy, New Jersey, Raritan River's first eastbound train of the day moves slowly uphill (Clegg, *Highball,* page 19). California State Railroad Museum, BC1151

5 Short Lines: "Not as Long but Just as Wide" 127

The Louisville, New Albany & Corydon carried passengers in its caboose between Corydon and Corydon Junction, Indiana. Passengers climb down from the caboose at Corydon (Clegg, top, *MTD,* page 326). At the junction, the Corydon's locomotive waits at the station (Clegg, facing page, *MTD,* page 326) for the arrival of the Southern Railway's train with passengers and express to transfer to the Corydon's caboose (Clegg, above). California State Railroad Museum, BC2797, BC2802, BC2808

The Morehead & North Fork's steam train runs from Clearfield, Kentucky, location of its home-like company office, to Morehead and a connection with the Chesapeake & Ohio. Clegg, California State Railroad Museum, BC2968

Manchester & Oneida, an eight-mile Iowa line, gives priority to track repairs in July 1946, forcing its steam train to wait until work is finished. Clegg, California State Railroad Museum, BC2961

Beebe labeled these photos "Along the Whisky Railroad," since the Frankfort & Cincinnati served various Kentucky distilleries, whisky-bottling works, and warehouses. A motor car picks up a passenger at Centerville, where the depot is located in G.A. Burberry's General Store (above). The car, M55-1, is preserved at the Kentucky Railway Museum, New Haven. Two hard-working engines are needed to pull and push a freight train out of the Frankfort yards and across the high trestle (facing page). The railroad connected Frankfort and Paris; it did not run to Cincinnati. It was "one of the few railroads in the world where the word 'highball' means anything but a signal for a clear track," Beebe concluded, referring, of course, to mixed drinks of whisky. Clegg, two photos, *MTD*, page 237, California State Railroad Museum, BC2142, BC2146

Hooppole, Yorktown & Tampico, a friendly line running through Illinois farmlands, often carried children free in its caboose. The photos here show its locomotive at the Hooppole Lumber & Grain Company grain elevator (right) and weed-grown right of way (below and facing page) in July 1946. Service ended in 1952. Clegg, three photos, California State Railroad Museum, BC2487, BC2495, BC2492

5 Short Lines: "Not as Long but Just as Wide" 135

Beebe and Clegg visited the Copper Range Railroad in Upper Michigan in August 1946. Clegg's photos show Beebe (above) next to their Buick convertible at the Houghton depot, conductor Pete Steinmetz, with Copper Range uniform and Milwaukee Road cap badge (facing page, above), and Beebe (facing page, bottom) along the track waving with camera in hand as the passenger train steams toward a connection with the Milwaukee Road's *Chippewa* at McKeever (Beebe is cropped out of the published version in *MTD,* page 252). Locomotive 29 and the second car are preserved at Mid-Continent Railway Historical Society, North Freedom, Wisconsin. The wartime train had only a few weeks to run; it operated from June 1, 1944, to September 15, 1946. Clegg, three photos California State Railroad Museum, BC0252, BC0253, BC0254

5 Short Lines: "Not as Long but Just as Wide" 137

Danville & Western mixed trains meet at a siding in Axton, Virginia (above, Clegg, *MTD,* page 64). California State Railroad Museum, BC1047

Dardanelle & Russellville in southwestern Arkansas carried passengers in January 1946 in its ex-Pennsylvania Railroad combine, with compartments "panelled in rare woods and decorated with carvings and joiner's handiwork," pulled by no. 11. Passengers get off the combine at Russellville (above). Beebe rides the combine with a D&R brakeman (facing page, *MTD,* page 95, Beebe is anonymous in the book). Clegg, two photos, California State Railroad Museum, BC0357, BC0355

Wichita Falls & Southern, an Oklahoma and Texas line, crossed the Texas & Pacific at Ranger, Texas. A sullen-appearing engine crew waits in the cab (above) while no. 30 takes on water in 1944–1945 (right), with Beebe at lower left. A similar photo, minus Beebe, appears in *Highball,* page 43. Clegg, California State Railroad Museum, BC0797, BC0803

Mixed Train Daily ignored the Morristown & Erie Railroad, which has been providing service to customers in New Jersey for more than a century (facing page). The water tank at Whippany, New Jersey, still stands today. Clegg, California State Railroad Museum, BC2849

Two standard-gauge Colorado short lines, at opposite ends of the state, present lonely and picturesque appearances. The Laramie, North Park & Western (Beebe, above and facing page, top) stretches south from a Union Pacific connection at Laramie, Wyoming, to Coalmont, Colorado. The San Luis Valley Southern extended from Blanca to the Colorado-New Mexico border at Jarosa. In October 1945, its crew works eight miles south of Blanca to put freight cars back on the track (Clegg, facing page, bottom) and its train turns on an isolated wye at Jarosa (Clegg, following two pages). California State Railroad Museum, BC2454, BC2455, BC1951, BC1955

Short lines dot the foothills of the western Sierra. Yosemite Valley eastbound mixed train no. 2 departs Merced Falls, California, en route to El Portal in 1945 (facing page, page 153, *The Age of Steam*, cropped as a vertical with the Merced River, highway bridge, and sawmill chopped out of the scene). Restrictions on logging outside Yosemite National Park led to the mill's closure in November 1942. A going-away shot of the same train following the Merced River east of Merced Falls appears in *MTD*, page 261. Locomotive no. 7 of another lumber line, the Amador Central, arrives at the station and office building in Martel, California, in 1944 with empty cars for the mill (above, *When Beauty Rode the Rails*, page 122). Clegg, two photos, California State Railroad Museum, BC0730, BC1464

Following two pages: Because of its steep grades, the Camino, Placerville & Lake Tahoe used Shay-type geared locomotives to haul lumber from the mill. A worker lubricates one of the locomotive's gears (*MTD*, page 281). Clegg, two photos, California State Railroad Museum, BC1331, BC1333

The historic Sierra Railroad Shops and Roundhouse at Railtown 1897, a California State Park in Jamestown, is one of the few remaining fully-operational original shortline roundhouse complexes in the country. Combine no. 5 was built for running on the tight curves and clearances of the Angels Branch. After the branch was abandoned in 1935, the car was used as a caboose into 1949. It was nicknamed "Mose's Caboose" in honor of longtime SRR trainman Mose Baker. (Clegg, facing page, above, *MTD,* page 304). The roundhouse stands ready to support the freight operations of a shortline railroad (Clegg, facing page, below). Then-retired 4-6-0 no. 3, on the left side of the photo, sat there throughout the 1930s and 1940s until Sierra restored it to operation in 1949. No. 3 then assumed all the movie jobs, most memorably in 1951's *High Noon.* A major restoration of no. 3 completed in 2010 keeps it going today, 126 years after rolling out of the Rogers factory in Paterson, New Jersey. Locomotive no. 34 heads the daily freight run from the lumber mills to the main-line connection at Oakdale (Clegg, above). Today, as Sierra Northern, the line serves rail customers along its forty-eight-mile route between Oakdale and Sonora. California State Railroad Museum, BC1993, BC1985, BC1991

6 On the Narrow Gauge

152　Beebe & Clegg: Their Enduring Photographic Legacy

Lucius Beebe and Charles Clegg admired narrow-gauge lines for their austere, down-home characteristics, but in southwestern Colorado they were able to organize a grand tour of the Rio Grande Southern in lavish style, with fine wines, full cooperation from railroad officials, and extensive press coverage.

Here and on other three-foot-gauge railroads they were collecting photographs and stories for their forthcoming book, *Mixed Train Daily*. In addition to the Rio Grande Southern, they chronicled the last of these lines in regular service: Denver & Rio Grande Western in Colorado and New Mexico, the East Broad Top in Pennsylvania, the East Tennessee & Western North Carolina, the Southern Pacific in the Owens Valley of California, and the Sumpter Valley in Oregon.

The Denver & Rio Grande Western was the most extensive and developed of the various narrow-gauge lines. In 1946 it played host to a legendary tour of its tracks and those of the connecting RGS. Beyond their research and photography, Beebe and Clegg used the journey as an opportunity to network and promote themselves and their work. It was also an opulent farewell to a fading era.

For the tour, Alfred E. Perlman, the Denver & Rio Grande Western's chief engineer (later, executive vice president of the Rio Grande and president of the New York Central and Western Pacific), served as host and furnished two ornate, narrow-gauge business cars for their trip. The D&RGW assigned Theodore von Dickersohn (1891–1968), the chef from the business car of Judge Wilson McCarthy (trustee of the railroad) and steward

Denver & Rio Grande Western's Silverton mixed train steams along the Animas River of Colorado in October 1946 in the days when it carried more freight than passengers. Today, the Durango & Silverton operates tourist trains on the forty-five miles. Clegg, with Beebe's camera, California State Railroad Museum, BC1559

6 On the Narrow Gauge 153

William Reed, to the train. They were fully capable of providing service in Beebe's grand signature style.[1]

The event began on September 30 with an elegant dinner in Denver. The group departed that night on a standard-gauge train bound for Alamosa. Pasquale "Pocky" Marranzino (1917–1998), columnist for Denver's *Rocky Mountain News,* provided daily narratives, reviewing the high points of the trip in five articles.[2] Marranzino, who wrote about Perlman for *Progressive Railroading,*[3] helped Beebe enlist Perlman's support for the trip.

Newspapers in Durango and Telluride also covered the trip as it was taking place. The RGS was so isolated there were no other newspapers along its route.[4]

The Rio Grande carried business cars B-2 and B-7 from Alamosa to Durango at the rear of its narrow-gauge passenger train, the *San Juan.* Conductor Henry Hines, who was beginning his fiftieth year with the company, regaled the attendees with stories of narrow-gauge railroading.

The 162-mile RGS portion of the trip began on October 2 and lasted three days, with overnight stops in Dolores and Telluride. The cars were part of a mixed train, with freight cars at the front of the train. RGS no. 20 pulled the train from Durango to Rico; the train crew included John H. Crum, conductor; Winfield Laube, engineer; George Thomas, fireman; and Andrew W. Sporer and Clark I. Thomas, brakemen. A leased D&RGW engine, no. 452, took the train the rest of the way from Rico to Telluride and on to Ridgway, with crew members Jay C. Phillips, conductor; Carl E. Quist, engineer; Mike S. Smith, fireman; and Frank Rasmussen and Claude Smith, brakemen. Clayton W. Graebing, RGS general manager, accompanied the train.

Beebe and Clegg carefully recognized local leaders along their route. In Durango they gave a formal dinner in honor of Alfred P. Camp, president of the First National Bank. (A building at Fort Lewis College is named for Camp.) For Camp's dinner, "the wonderfully ornate silver kerosene lamp in the dining car was lighted, the caviar chilled, and the table meticulously set with the very best Rio Grande silver service."

The cars were parked near the D&RGW depot, now headquarters for the Durango & Silverton Narrow Gauge Railroad, which operates the only surviving trackage out of the city, the famous Animas Canyon route to Silverton.

When writing about the first day on the narrow gauge, Marranzino said Beebe, "the Homer of American railroads, was drooling over the magic of this almost miniature train. He didn't miss a stop, perusing every inch of our 75-year-old coach and the entire length of the train."

The next day—the first on the Rio Grande Southern—the train roared into Dolores "as the sun made a spectacular setting over the San Juan Mountains." It had taken eight hours to take six empty stock cars, caboose, and two business cars the sixty miles from Durango, "but to go faster than that through the amazingly beautiful country would be sacrilegious."

The second RGS day, the train pulled out of Dolores following the Galloping Goose, a motor car which provided the RGS's mail and passenger service. At Rico, thirty-five miles away, Navajo tribe members met the train with a ceremonial dance. Beebe and Clegg arranged for the actress and politician Elizabeth Pellet (1887–1976) to meet them at

Beebe, holding Clegg's Medalist camera, stands outside the station at Chama, New Mexico, with Division Superintendent L. H. Hale and conductor Henry Hines. California State Railroad Museum, BC3790

Rico. (She performed on stage and in movies, and served eighteen years in the Colorado legislature.) Pellet explained that most children had never seen a train with sleeping cars, so school was called off.[5]

The train left at noon, winding through "the Switzerland of Colorado" to Lizard Head Pass and on to the "storybook" mining town of Ophir.

After spending the night at Telluride, the travelers went to Ridgway in rain and snow squalls. "The low-hanging clouds and muggy weather irked Beebe and his associate, Charles Clegg, who have been having a photographic holiday along the quaint line with its breath-taking scenery," Marranzino wrote. They left the RGS at Ridgway and continued on D&RGW narrow-gauge track. "The broad gauge of Montrose track looked unbelievably wide after four days of the slim iron. It seemed a little depressing as we watched the little narrow gauge engine pull out of the Montrose yard. She whistled a forlorn goodbye after she had disappeared out of sight trailed by a tottering caboose." The group returned to Denver in a standard-gauge business car.

Robert W. Richardson, longtime director of the Colorado Railroad Museum, recalled years later that RGS crews worried about the heavy business cars. "The car foreman when asked said all he knew was the cars were heavier than the regular passenger cars [on] account [of] having extra sills," he wrote.[6]

The D&RGW's company publication, the *Green Light,* joked about the trip. "At nightfall, in the shadow of majestic Lizard Head, Lucius carefully adjusted his top hat, white tie, and tails, and majestically beckoned for Chef Theodore von Dickersohn to bring on the caviar and trimmin's." Perlman balked at the tails and dressed in a business suit.[7]

Time summarized the trip in a slightly sarcastic report: "Lucius Beebe, U.S. journalism's most rococo columnist, went digging for facts in Colorado, after his fashion. To mine material for another nostalgic book about his hobby, railroads, locomotive-loco Lucius, assisted only by his Manhattan roommate, a photographer, and a small, hardy retinue, braved narrow-gauge trails in a private railroad car."[8]

Beebe wrote his own account in the *New York Herald Tribune.* "If this was to be the last journey of the little cars over the historic run it was, in any event, accomplished in the grand manner," he said.[9] Coverage of their sentimental journey was far-reaching, from *Railway Age* to *Railroad* magazine.[10] *Trains* published a photo and wrote that the trip on the RGS attracted "widespread attention as the first steam passenger train with sleeping cars to run over the narrow gauge rails since 1899."[11]

They had photographed the RGS several times, but this was their only trip in passenger cars. The railroad ceased operations in December 1951 and the ICC formally approved abandonment the next year. *Trains* suggested it become a railroad national monument.[12]

Beebe turned the trip into a money-making opportunity, writing "Narrow-Gauge Holiday" about the *San Juan* and Silverton branch passenger service for *Holiday.*[13]

In 1949, this time without Clegg, Beebe again traveled the narrow gauge with the John W. Barriger III and Alfred Perlman families in a single car.

"On Labor Day weekend in 1949, we joined the Perlmans and Beebe at Pueblo on board D&RGW 115. We went on the narrow gauge from Alamosa to Durango and Silverton. From Durango we flew to Denver (my first flight), then took CB&Q 10 to Chicago," recalled Stanley Barriger, son of John III.

"When Beebe arrived at Durango, he put on his top hat and his cutaway and his mouse colored waistcoat with gold watch chain, walked into the bar at the Strater Hotel, propped himself up on a stool, and held court for the next three to four hours. It was quite a sight. He was a very big man, with his top hat and cutaway outfit, he cut quite a figure. The place was jammed all evening," according to John W. "Jack" Barriger IV.

Perlman was trying to abandon the narrow gauge lines. "But this was an opportunity to do something that was fun, and there was a narrow gauge business car. Perlman and his wife, Adele, and Dad and Mother, and Beebe filled up the dinner table." Jack, then a student at MIT, recalled with a laugh how "Beebe walked back to the observation end, saw me starting lunch with my brothers and sisters, turned his nose up as only Beebe could, and said, 'I see you have to eat in the steerage.'"[14]

Beebe and Clegg did not dedicate as much print space to the other narrow-gauge lines, but they treated them with the same tender loving care.

At the Sumpter Valley, a lumber line in Oregon, they photographed two massive 2-6-6-2 type Mallet locomotives, originally built for the Uintah Railway of Utah, and a tiny diesel switcher.

Beebe recounted stories about derailments, adding a light touch to his text. When three cars loaded with beer and whiskey for the "thirsty lumberjacks" of Bates got away on a curve, the derailment "gladdened the countryside for days." Another time, cars of cattle derailed between Sumpter and Larch. The railroad hired "professional cowpokes" to round up the cattle at $5 a head. "The buckaroos, thus enflamed with cupidity, set about their task with prodigious enthusiasm and turned into the astonished railroad officials 100 more cattle than were known to have escaped from the cars," Beebe wrote.[15]

The original track was scrapped in 1947, and nearly all of the original roadbed eroded away. A restoration began on January 4, 1971, when the Sumpter Valley Railroad Restoration was incorporated, only twenty-four years after the original railway had stopped operations. The people in Baker County never forgot the "Stump Dodger." With an almost all-volunteer work force, the SVRy has rebuilt more than seven miles of track and is still growing.[16]

The Tweetsie, or East Tennessee & Western North Carolina, described as "a rare, dainty, and proud narrow gauge," operated between Johnson City, Tennessee, and Cranberry, North Carolina. (Earlier it had gone to Boone, North Carolina.) The trains operated on dual-gauge track between Johnson City and Elizabethton.

On the October day when Beebe and Clegg visited, no. 12's locomotive crew showed off an "understandably ungracious possum" they caught that morning and were keeping in the tool box of the locomotive cab. The railroad "served a region calculated in itself to arouse a warmth of admiration: the fiercely individualistic and altogether independent Grandfather Mountain country," according to *Mixed Train Daily*.[17]

The last revenue train ran October 16, 1950, and the rails were pulled up in 1951. Service to Elizabethton ended in 2003, but a successor, East Tennessee Railway, still handles local Johnson City traffic. No. 12, after a short time away, in 1957 returned to the "Tweetsie Railroad," an amusement park a few miles from the end of the old line at Boone, where it operates today.

The narrow-gauge section in the Doe River Gorge had been the scenic centerpiece of a trip on the line. In the late 1960s, about two and a half miles of rail were relaid on the gorge right of way and a train ran for a few years as part of an amusement park. Doe River Gorge Ministries, Hampton, Tennessee, acquired the property in 1987. Today, motorcars with their trailers and a diesel train provide access to the gorge.[18]

In true Beebe fashion, Beebe and Clegg gave priority to the passenger operations of the East Broad Top in Pennsylvania—the coach on its mixed train, morning and night shuttle trains taking coal miners to work and back home, and a business car once used by President Grover Cleveland for fishing parties in Maine. They ignored the line's significant coal traffic and its historic machine shop.[19]

The EBT has been a National Historic Landmark since 1964. The line winds through thirty-one miles of mountain scenery and remains virtually intact, including track, steam locomotives, cars and facilities. The railroad abandoned operations in 1956 and was purchased by the Kovalchick family, known for their extensive scrapping operations. The

Rio Grande Southern no. 20 rolls the Beebe-Clegg special across the meadows above Dolores in southwestern Colorado. Clegg, *MTD*, page 154, and *Age of Steam*, page 207. California State Railroad Museum, BC3238

6 On the Narrow Gauge 157

Examples from Rio Grande Southern photos show Clegg's hand-written instructions about how he wanted photos printed. California State Railroad Museum, BCP3064, BCP3310

family returned five miles to operation as a tourist line. It has been closed since December 2011 but remains intact. Volunteers of the Friends of the East Broad Top continue working to stabilize the buildings and equipment.

Southern Pacific's operations in the Owens Valley of California received heavy coverage because it was a remnant of the Carson & Colorado, a railroad initially associated with Nevada's Virginia & Truckee. The C&C, incorporated in 1880, connected with the V&T at Mound House, east of Carson City. It reached Keeler, California, in 1883. Beebe and Clegg quoted an investor, Darius Ogden Mills, who was not impressed after a tour of the line, said, "they had built the railroad 300 miles too long, or 300 years too soon."[20] In 1900 its investors sold the line to the Southern Pacific. Two months after the sale, silver and gold discoveries at Tonopah, Nevada, and later in Goldfield, Nevada, in 1904 created unheard-of traffic levels. The SP standard-gauged the northern 140 miles from Mound House to Mina, Nevada, in 1905. The section between Mina and Laws was abandoned in 1938; operations ceased entirely in 1960.[21]

In 2016 the all-volunteer Carson & Colorado Railway restored no. 18 to operating condition. The locomotive, originally built for the Nevada-California-Oregon Railroad as its no. 12, remained on the N-C-O's roster until 1926, when the Southern Pacific bought the railroad and converted it to standard gauge. The SP transferred the locomotive to the SP's three-foot-gauge lines in Nevada and California and renumbered it as their no. 18.

Retired by the railroad in 1954 and put on display in Independence, California, in 1955, the 1911 Baldwin sat until 1997 when the group began a campaign to restore it. The group takes its name from the original C&C railroad and plans to run the locomotive at narrow gauge operations throughout the country.

Today, people fondly remember all of these properties. They are preserved in one way or another or rebuilt as tourist railroads, a recognition of Clegg and Beebe's ability to pick historic, significant places to feature in their books.

Notes

1. Gruber, "Beebe & Clegg Ride the Rio Grande Southern," *Classic Trains*, Fall 2016, 32-37.
2. Pasquale Marranzino, *Rocky Mountain News*, Oct. 1-5, 1946.
3. Marranzino, "Perlman of the Rio Grande," *Railway Progress*, Aug. 1948, 25-26.
4. "Narrow Gauge Trip, Dinner by Lamplight, Give Columnist, Party Flashback to '80s," *Durango Herald-Democrat*, Oct. 2, 1946; "Rico Gives Newsmen Big Reception" and "Newsmen Visit City on Narrow Gauge Passenger Cars, *Telluride (Colo.) Tribune*, Oct. 10, 1946.
5. "Elizabeth Eyre Pellet, Colorado Women's Hall of Fame, inducted 2016, http://www.cogreatwomen.org/project/elizabeth-eyre-pellet/
6. Robert W. Richardson to Gruber, Dec. 20, 2006.
7. "Lucius, Caviar, and Tails Rough It on the Southern," *Green Light*, D&RGW Railroad, Oct. 15, 1946.
8. "People," *Time*, Oct. 14, 1946, 44.
9. Beebe, "Narrow Gauge Train Steams Into Yesterday," *Herald Tribune*, Oct. 13, 1946.
10. "Mixed Train Daily," *Railroad*, Feb. 1947, 39-45; and "Rio Grande Southern 'Recorded' Before Abandonment," *Railway Age*, Nov. 9, 1946, 775.
11. *Trains*, December 1946, 5, 8.
12. *Trains*, July 1962, 10.
13. Beebe, "Narrow-Gauge Holiday," *Holiday*, March 1947, 81-83.
14. John W. "Jack" Barriger IV and Stanley Barriger, "Barriger's Unique Visual Record," *Railroad Heritage* 2 (2000), 4; Jack Barriger at *Conversations 2016* conference in Lake Forest, Illinois, and "Recollections of Lucius Beebe," letter to Gruber, April 27, 2016.
15. Sumpter Valley, "Less than Carload Lots," *Mixed Train Daily*, 309-318.
16. Sumpter Valley Railroad, http://sumptervalleyrailroad.org/index.html.
17, Tweetsie, "Our Little Train," *Mixed Train Daily*, 75-83,
18. "Railroad History," Doe River Gorge Ministries, http://www.doerivergorge.com/railroad/history.php.
19. "Pennsylvania's Strait-Gauge Railroad," *Mixed Train Daily*, 206, also 297-299.
20. Beebe and Clegg, *Virginia & Truckee*, 38; *Mixed Train Daily*, 212.
21. Carson & Colorado Railroad, Pacific Coast Narrow Gauge, http://pacificng.com/template.php?page=roads/nv/cc/index.htm

Narrow Gauge Kingdom

Clegg's photo of the Durango, Colorado, roundhouse, "the hub of narrow gauge world in the United States," introduces "Narrow Gauge Kingdom," an expansive section of *Mixed Train Daily*. The text begins with a ballad by Powder River Jack Lee, "In Durango, In Durango / The Spaniards did fandango." Beebe and Clegg expressed lavish praise for the lines running on rails three feet apart (*MTD*, page 112; *Age of Steam*, page 204). Today, no. 346 is the superstar of the Colorado Railroad Museum at Golden. California State Railroad Museum, BC3229

On the facing page, the D&RGW's twice-a-week mixed train to Silverton approaches Granite Point, which sits on the ledge above Shalona Lake, coming into Rockwood. Clegg took the photo about 1945 for *Mixed Train Daily* (page 156), *Age of Steam* (page 202), and *Hear the Train Blow* (page 225). Today, the Durango & Silverton Narrow Gauge Railroad operates many round trips on this line at the peak of its summer season. It is a National Historic Landmark and a National Historic Civil Engineering Landmark. California State Railroad Museum, BC3240

The Daily *San Juan*

Beebe and Clegg sometimes displayed photos in different ways in different books. Beebe's photo here shows the *San Juan*, the last daily, narrow-gauge passenger train in the U.S. carrying a deluxe parlor-observation car, with locomotive 478 in October 1945 near Durango. No. 478 climbs the grade outside Durango and crosses the state highway in a vertical view *(MTD,* page 171). *Narrow Gauge in the Rockies* (page 59) and *The Age of Steam* (page 210) show the picture as a horizontal view. The full negative reproduced here is more impressive than the published pictures. California State Railroad Museum, BC1541

The westbound *San Juan* waits at Carracas, Colorado, as a freight train "saws by" in a view from the back platform of the eastbound *San Juan* (facing page, above), and the eastbound drifts along the Animas River south of Durango (facing page, below). Beebe, two photos, California State Railroad Museum, BC1570, BC1572

6 On the Narrow Gauge 163

Narrow-gauge freights ran from Durango, Colorado, south to Farmington, New Mexico, and east to Chama, New Mexico, and then on to Alamosa, Colorado. In these October 1945 scenes, a double header is on its way to Chama (top). On the Farmington Branch, a train passes the depot at Aztec, New Mexico (above). Clegg climbed the hillside for an unusual and uncharacteristic view high above the train at Bondad Hill, Colorado (facing page). Clegg, three photos, California State Railroad Museum, BC1528, BC1540, BC1561

Elegant Travel on the Rio Grande Southern

At dinner in Durango aboard D&RGW car B-2 are (clockwise from left foreground) Charles Clegg, Pasquale "Pocky" Marranzino, bank president Alfred P. Camp, RGS General Manager Clayton W. Graebing, Lucius Beebe, Durango *Herald Democrat* editor Harold L. Anderson, Durango chamber of commerce president Clair Campbell, D&RGW Chief Engineer Alfred E. Perlman, and D&RGW Alamosa Division superintendent L. H. Hale. (Clegg, above, by timer). Wherever the Beebe/Clegg special traveled on the Rio Grande Southern in 1946, people turned out. Business cars and celebrities were seldom seen on the remote line. At Rico, Beebe, Elizabeth Pellet, and Pasquale "Pocky" Marranzino pose (facing page, top, left), while children were allowed to leave school to see the train (facing page, top, right). At Lizard Head Pass, the train made one of its many stops, with the front in the snow shed (facing page, below). Clegg, four photos, California State Railroad Museum, BCP4022, BC3250, BC3258, BC3248

6 On the Narrow Gauge 167

Rio Grande Southern used two locomotives for the special, which Clegg referred to as "our train" on his proof prints. At Ophir station in Colorado, the shaft of its principal mine is visible (Clegg, facing page, top, *MTD*, page 150). With no. 452, leased from the D&RGW, pulling the train, it crosses a wooden trestle leaving Ophir (Beebe, above). No. 20, seen at Dolores, traveled as far as Rico (Beebe, facing page, bottom). California State Railroad Museum, BC3023, BC3047, BC3063

Rio Grande Southern's Lonely Freight Service

Rio Grande Southern provided freight service, usually twice a week. With its own locomotive no. 20 on the front and double-headed with no. 452, leased from the D&RGW, the train crosses Lightner Creek Trestle west of Durango (Clegg, above, *MTD,* page 131). Later, it rolls along through a river valley (Clegg, facing page, top). On another day, no. 452 leads a train with a helper engine cut in the middle (Beebe, facing page, bottom, *MTD,* page 142). Schenectady built no. 20 for the Florence & Cripple Creek in 1899. California State Railroad Museum, BC1170, BC3320, BC3314

Rio Grande Southern's fleet of home-built Galloping Geese provided mail, express, and passenger service. Goose No. 4 pulls out of Dolores, Colorado, early in the morning (Beebe, above, *MTD*, page 143). Native Americans board the Goose at Rico, riding to Vance Junction (Clegg, facing page, above, *MTD*, page 144). At Lizard Head Pass, the Goose stops at the deserted depot (Clegg, above, *MTD* page 147). No. 4 now is on display at Telluride. California State Railroad Museum BC3066, BC3322, BC3024

Rio Grande Southern no. 20 heads east at Mancos, Colorado (above), where an RGS brakeman is shown "bending the iron" (right, *MTD*, page 139). He is wearing a "thousand-miler shirt," which Beebe wrote comes from the tradition "that its material contains so little white that it can be worn a thousand miles between launderings." Beebe, two photos, California State Railroad Museum, BC3053, BC3207

When Beebe and Clegg visited Telluride, Colorado, in 1946, it was a sleepy former mining town. Today, Telluride is a thriving mountain community, with a host of ski resorts, festivals, and music and performing arts events. The U.S. Department of the Interior designated its central area as a National Historic Landmark District in 1961. Clegg, *MTD*, page 152, California State Railroad Museum, BC3027

Oregon's Sumpter Valley

The Sumpter Valley, the last of the narrow-gauge common carriers in the northwest, operated in the Blue Mountains of Oregon. Its Mallet locomotive brings finished lumber to its interchange with the Union Pacific at Baker (Beebe, *Age of Steam,* page 173). California State Railroad Museum, BC2053

Clegg and Beebe stood nearby one another along the track near McEwen yet took strikingly different photos of the Sumpter Valley a few seconds apart. Clegg (top, *Age of Steam*, page 173) shows more of the landscape, while Beebe (above, *MTD*, page 317) produced an "in your face" view of the locomotive and train. Both used Kodak Medalist cameras, unusual for Beebe. California State Railroad Museum, BC3330, BC2063

Sumpter Valley's no. 256, a Mallet built for the Uintah Railway of Utah, stops for water (Beebe, top) and crosses the Powder River on a low trestle on its way to the Union Pacific connection at Baker (Clegg, above, *MTD,* page 215). California State Railroad Museum, BC2052, BC3323

Cattle graze next to the Sumpter Valley's unfenced right of way (Clegg). California State Railroad Museum, BC3350

Southern Pacific in Owens Valley

Southern Pacific narrow gauge 4-6-0 no. 18, leaving Laws, California (Clegg, above, *MTD*, page 219), returned to operation in 2017 at Dehy Park in nearby Independence, California. Built by Baldwin in 1911, the SP retired no. 18 in 1954 and put the locomotive on display in Independence 1955. In 1997 the all-volunteer Carson & Colorado Railway began a campaign to restore it; work was completed in 2016. The group takes its name from the original railroad that operated here. SP's Owens Valley branch was what was left of the original C&C. No. 8 runs along an arm of the Panamint Mountains (Beebe, facing page, above, *MTD*, page 215). The going away view shows details of the catwalk that has been added to the C&C combine (Beebe, facing page, below, *MTD*, page 218). California State Railroad Museum, BC1260, BC1112, BC1259

Southern Pacific 4-6-0 no. 18, with only an auxiliary water car and combine, blasts upgrade into Laws, California, the northern end of the narrow-gauge run, in June 1946 (*MTD,* page 211). Water stops at Keeler were routine (facing page). Clegg, two photos, California State Railroad Museum, BC1114, BC1222

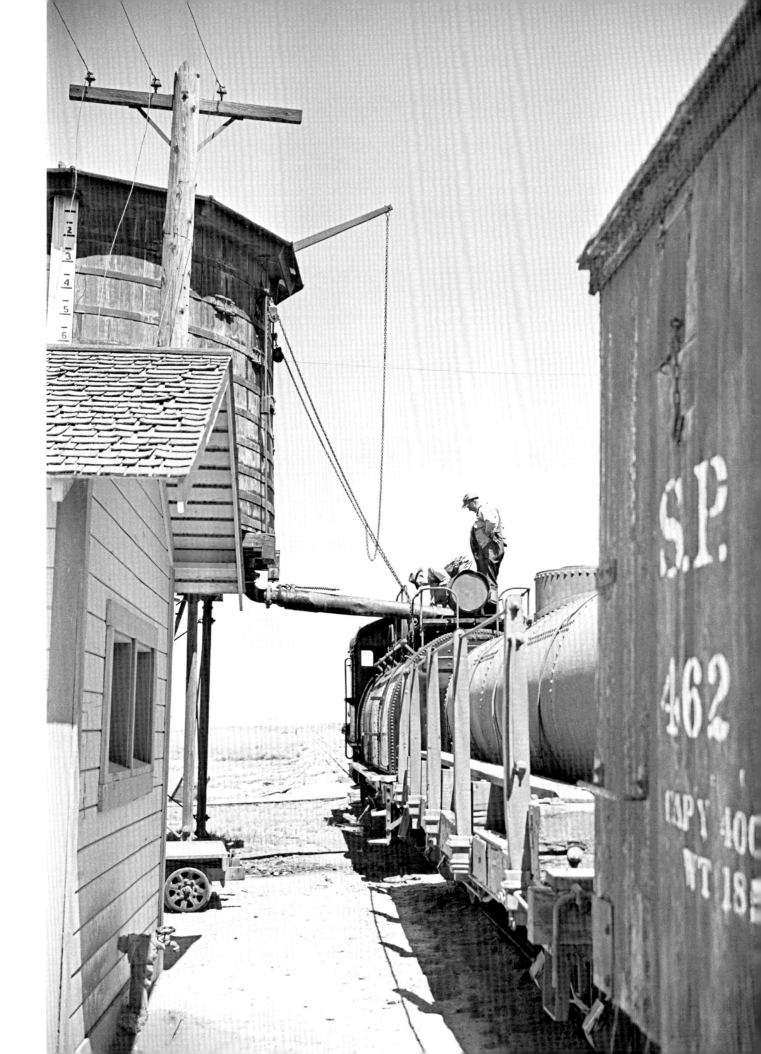

At Owenyo, workers move cargo from narrow- to standard-gauge cars (above, *MTD,* page 218). In a superb informal portrait, conductor James A. Brennan (1903–1966) smiles at his desk in the Carson & Colorado combine which serves as a caboose (facing page, *MTD,* page 220). Brennan worked for the SP from 1941 to 1965. Clegg, two photos, California State Railroad Museum, BC1219, BC1196

East Broad Top

At the East Broad Top in Pennsylvania, coal moved in standard-gauge hopper cars (Clegg, facing page; Beebe, top). The railroad connected with the Pennsylvania Railroad at Mount Union, where interchanged freight car's trucks were changed from standard to narrow gauge for the thirty-three-mile run south into the coal fields. East Broad Top's passenger trains carried miners to work. Beebe is shown on the right shortly after taking a photo (Clegg, above). California State Railroad Museum, BC2711, BC2692, BC2695

Tweetsie

The East Tennessee & Western North Carolina, locally known as "Tweetsie," served a rural countryside, well described by its name. Clegg and Beebe visited in 1946. Locomotive no. 12 pulls a train up a grade in mountainous terrain (facing page). Wooden cars are on the ground at Elk Park, North Carolina (top). No 12 leads a narrow-gauge train passes the Bemburg Rayon Plant on the edge of Elizabethton, Tennessee, on the dual-gauge track between Elizabethton and Johnson City, Tennessee, where the Tweetsie connected with the Southern and Clinchfield. No. 12 today operates at the Tweetsie Railroad theme park in Blowing Rock, North Carolina. (above, *MTD*, page 79). Clegg, three photos, California State Railroad Museum, BC3088, BC2246, BC2753

East Tennessee & Western North Carolina switch stands from the Linnville River branch stand at Johnson City, Tennessee, waiting to be scrapped (Clegg, right, *MTD*, page 78). Dramatic lighting shows part of a train on a heavy grade (Clegg, below). The train crew shows off, inhumanely, an opossum they are carrying to town in the tool box in the locomotive cab (Clegg, facing page). California State Railroad Museum, BC2751, BC2241, BC2748

7 Nevada and the Virginia & Truckee

Nevada's Virginia & Truckee Railroad embodied all the classic Beebe and Clegg elements—especially their mutual love of the Old West and traditional steam railroading. Although they photographed other Nevada mining railroads, the V&T remained their all-time favorite.

The V&T opened from Virginia City to Carson City in 1869 to serve the Comstock Lode, then was extended north to Reno in 1872 and south to Minden in 1906. The line between Carson City and Virginia City was abandoned in 1938.

In 1946, while gathering material for *Mixed Train Daily,* Beebe and Clegg arranged for steam locomotives Nos. 25 and 26 to be on the regular train from Carson City to Minden with all of the V&T's passenger equipment and the line's club car. With approval of general manager Gordon A. Sampson (1888–1980), a former comptroller for Columbia Pictures, the railroad turned over the train to Beebe and Clegg, who spent several hours

192 Beebe & Clegg: Their Enduring Photographic Legacy

photographing in the Carson Valley, according to the *Reno Gazette-Journal*.[1]

Beebe and Clegg were smitten with the V&T. They spent the summers of 1948 to 1950 living and writing in their private car, the *Gold Coast*, under a cottonwood tree on a V&T siding in Carson City. All was not work. When writers and train enthusiasts paid them a visit, they would hook their car on the train to Reno for a night of gambling and floor shows at the Mapes Hotel.

A double-headed train on the Virginia & Truckee climbs a grade just outside Carson City on the run to Minden, Nevada, in what appears to be a photo runby for the authors. For Beebe and Clegg, the V&T was a favorite railroad, but they were not able to save it from abandonment. Clegg, California State Railroad Museum, BC1446

Nevada Copper Belt no. 5, recently purchased by the V&T, takes the daily mixed train from Reno to Carson City and Minden in fall 1947 (Beebe, right, *MTD,* page 217; *Age of Steam,* page 133). At Douglas, Nevada, the train from Reno on the Carson City-Minden branch passes an abandoned section house. Giant trees about five times as tall as the locomotive dwarf the train. This is an exceptional image, wedding a dramatic landscape with a small train emitting an iconic and giant plume of black smoke. Today the tracks are gone but the buildings and trees still stand (Clegg, below, *MTD,* page 209). California State Railroad Museum, BC3039, BC3133

During the winter, Beebe lived in New York and continued writing for the *Herald Tribune*, whose owners, the Reid family (descendants of Darius Ogden Mills, 1825–1910, a builder of the railroad and a president of the Bank of California), also owned the V&T. Beebe tried to convince the owners of the newspaper to save the railroad. He arranged for an editorial in the *Herald Tribune*, optimistically declaring that a revival was beginning: "Many and many a person quite indifferent to railroad affairs in general will rejoice for the V&T because it is an active and tangible survivor of the old times in the glamorous West of fiction when all the world was young."[2]

Enthusiasm did not pay the bills, and in one of the great disappointments of Beebe's life, he could not change the decision to scrap the railroad.

In somewhat breathless fashion, in a fruitless last gasp to save the line, Beebe and Clegg wrote *Virginia & Truckee: A Story of Virginia City and Comstock Times*.[3] The book was the first published by Grahame H. Hardy, an Oakland book dealer, resulting in a continuing series of correspondence between Beebe, Clegg, and Hardy.

"The copy is in the works. I spent Labor Day on it with occasional recourse to a slight sip of champagne which I find refreshes the creative mind, until I fell out of my chair. I'll probably have it for the compositor by the turn of the year," Beebe wrote in September from New York.[4]

Sampson, general manager of the V&T, evidently wanted a significant say-so about the book and the authors disagreed. "I don't know what he can contribute to the book that we do not already know but I am perfectly agreeable to letting him think he has a finger in it if that will make him happy," Beebe wrote.[5]

In his "last word" on Sampson, Beebe said, after talking with Clegg, "in a few days I will forward you the final draft which will put an end to this entire offensive imbroglio. It will be substantially as it stands at the moment except that I shall be at pains to eliminate any editorial opinions of the authors and quote only from the established record … . Chuck and I are agreed that we made a major tactical error when we even discussed the matter with Sampson in the first place when I was West and I have better things to do than nurse this character's sick delusions of grandeur and importance," Beebe said.[6]

Beebe was not happy with the Reid family, but did not want to offend them. "I had lunch with Mrs. [Helen] Reid the other day and she was somewhat upset about the V&T book, although she laughed at … part but was hurt by the statement that profits had been taken from the railroad and that Whitelaw Reid was owner of the *Tribune*. He is editor and co-owner with her, for the record. I pointed out that the profits part had been corrected and produced a copy, happily at hand, to prove it," Beebe told Hardy. Beebe hurriedly asked Clegg and Hardy to "cut or reword any indelicate lines."[7]

The first edition appeared in April 1949. "This is the story of a railroad so endowed with romance and wealthy destinies as to have become a legend in its own lifetime, an integral portion of the greatest of all pioneering sagas, the *matiere* of the old American West," Beebe and Clegg wrote in their introduction.[8] The book was serialized in the *Reno*

Arnold "Bill" Fryk "assumes the immemorial pose of an old-time engineer." Unfortunately, he never worked for the V&T (Beebe, *Age of Steam*, page 129; *When Beauty Rode the Rails*, page 81). Beebe referred to Fryk (1912–1976) as "High Water Bill," although he was more commonly known as "Bad Water Bill." Dressed as a prospector, Fryk with his burro became a celebrity in Virginia City. A statue in Sparks, *Last Chance Joe*, is based on his profile. Beebe, California State Railroad Museum, BC3413

The V&T's McKeen Car, listed on the National Register of Historic Places in 2005, is a self-propelled gasoline engine car built by the McKeen Motor Car Company of Omaha, Nebraska. The V&T operated it from 1910 to 1945, running well over 500,000 miles in service. Beebe disliked the car, but photographed it at Reno (facing page, top). It is meticulously restored and occasionally operates at the Nevada State Railroad Museum in Carson City. The official unveiling of the restored car was May 9, 2010, one hundred years exactly from the date it was delivered to the V&T. The V&T mixed runs next to a city street in Carson City (facing page, bottom). A train exits Washoe Canyon, a favorite and frequently photographed location on the V&T (above). Beebe, three photos, California State Railroad Museum, BC1394, BC1677, BC1298

Evening Gazette beginning April 25.[9] By June, it was so popular that a new, enlarged fourth edition had been ordered.[10]

Years later, Sampson had modified his opinion of the work and autographed a copy for Cathlyn Hammes Mowbray of Las Vegas, wife of John Mowbray, Nevada Supreme Court Justice, "as a slight token of my appreciation for her interest in Virginia City, Nevada, the birthplace of the railway."[11]

Beebe wrote *Life* magazine about covering the last trip. "Several senior editors, notably John Billings, are entirely railroad conscious," he told Hardy.[12] John Jenkisson of *Life* quickly expressed interest, but there was no coverage.[13]

As the end approached, Sampson decided he would not permit the *Gold Coast* to be on the last train, so the partners had to move it off the V&T and to Sparks, Nevada, earlier than hoped. "Two weeks before abandonment, I considered it advisable to request Mr. Lucius Beebe and his photographic associate, Mr. Charles Clegg, to ship out their private Pullman in order to avoid any accident at the last moment. Of course, it had been Mr. Beebe's intention to have his Pullman on the rear of the last train in order that he might receive the plaudits of the cheering public. Whether he would have assumed the attire of an early western gambler, silk top hat, et al, and have had Mr. Clegg dress up in a true replica of Sherlock Holmes, I cannot say." Sampson wrote.

The V&T moved the car on May 16, but it could not be on the rear of train. "The consist was comprised of but two empty boxcars, and to have placed this heavy piece of equipment at the rear could, in all likelihood, cause the boxcars to become derailed. It therefore became necessary to couple the Pullman directly to the engine tender with the boxcars and Coach no. 18 in the rear. Thus the outgoing presented somewhat of a sorry appearance, but it was the best that could be done under the circumstances."[14]

Sampson cited "all the confusion and the celebrations instant to the last run" as a reason but the last day was calm. "Few witness the last departure of local train," the *Reno Evening Gazette* wrote on its front page. The formal farewell was reserved for the school children at Steamboat.[15]

For the last day, Beebe went to his favorite location at Lakeview, on the ridge overlooking Washoe Valley, for a final photograph. The coverage in the *Herald Tribune* was short, without embellishment.[16]

Clegg later wrote a tribute to the V&T which was published in *American Heritage* in 1953. It covered the same topics Beebe would have covered but without the grandiose prose.

Beebe and Clegg were not the line's only photographers. Their V&T books include pictures by photographers such as Stanley G. Palmer, Roy D. Graves, Jim Morley, and Ted Wurm. Many others such as John Illman also photographed it. Their enthusiasm, and understanding of the V&T, enabled Beebe and Clegg to present more dramatic views than those taken by Arthur Rothstein of the Farm Security Administration-Office of War Information.

Beebe and Clegg expanded their coverage of Nevada to include other shortline railroads.[17] They photographed no. 5 on the Nevada Copper Belt, running between Hudson and Wabuska. The NCB was abandoned in 1947 and sold no. 5 to the V&T, where Beebe and Clegg would see it again on the V&T's daily mixed train.[18]

They also covered the Tonopah & Goldfield, which when built early in the 20th century was "the last great bonanza railroad of the even then fast vanishing American frontier." It remained busy through World War II hauling aviation gasoline to the Army Air Field at Tonopah, then was abandoned in 1947 around the same time *Mixed Train Daily* hit the book stands.[19]

In a more elaborate volume, *Steamcars to the Comstock* (1957), Beebe and Clegg concluded their V&T tribute in an uncharacteristic, simple statement: "Railroads such as the V. & T. do not die but live on in the hearts of men forever."

Notes

1. "Noted Photographer Takes V&T Pictures," *Reno Gazette-Journal,* June 13, 1946.
2. "New Life Comes to the V&T," *New York Herald Tribune,* Jan. 16, 1946, 22.
3. Beebe and Clegg, *Virginia & Truckee: A Story of Virginia City and Comstock Times* (Oakland, Calif.: Grahame H. Hardy, 1949).
4. Beebe to Hardy from New York City, Sept. 9, 1948. CSRM.
5. Beebe to Hardy from New York City, Jan. 9, 1949. CSRM.
6. Beebe to Hardy from New York City, July 16, 1949. CSRM.
7. Beebe to Hardy from New York City, March 25, 1950.
8. Beebe and Clegg, *Legends of the Comstock Lode* (Oakland, Calif.: Graham H. Hardy, 1950), 7.
9. "Virginia & Truckee." Reno Evening G*azette,* April 25, 1949.
10. "Fourth Edition of V&T Book," *Reno-Gazette Journal,* June 8,1949.
11. Gordon A. Sampson to Mowbry, April 22, 1959. John Gruber collection.
12. Beebe to Hardy from New York City, Jan. 17, 1949. CSRM.
13. John Jenkisson, *Life,* to Beebe, Jan. 18, 1949, CSRM.
14. Gordon A. Sampson, *Memoirs,* "The Return to Reno, Marriage, and the Years with the Virginia & Truckee Railway." University of Nevada Oral History Archive, 159.
15. "V&T Railroad, Nevada's Last Shortline, Quits Today," *Reno Evening Gazette,* May 31, 1950, 1.
16. "Virginia & Truckee Runs Its Last Train," *New York Herald Tribune,* June 1, 1950.
17. David F. Myrick, *Railroads of Nevada and Eastern Nevada,* vol. 1 (Berkeley, Calif: Howell-North, 1962) has details about these and other railroads in the area.
18. "Sunset on the Nevada Copper Belt," *Mixed Train Daily,* 217.
19. "Last of the Bonanza Railroads," *Mixed Train Daily,* 222.

In a going-away photo in 1950, Clegg shows the V&T in a classic pictorial view of the train and landscape *(Age of Steam,* page 121). California State Railroad Museum, BC1438

V&T no. 26, a Railway Post Office car, and a combine round a curve near Lakeview in an unusual hillside perspective. The photo appeared in *Trains* magazine in a pre-publication article about *Mixed Train Daily*. Beebe, *MTD,* page 200. David P. Morgan Library, Kalmbach Publishing Co.

7 Nevada and the Virginia & Truckee 201

Tonopah & Goldfield

A doubleheaded mixed train on the T&G crosses the Nevada desert under a July sun near Tonopah Junction. It carries a Pullman from San Francisco (Beebe, above, *Highball,* page 38). All trains bring aviation gas to the Army Airfield at Tonopah (Clegg, facing page, top; Clegg, facing page, bottom, *MTD,* page 224). Built in 1905, "it was the last great bonanza railroad of the even then fast vanishing American frontier," Beebe wrote. California State Railroad Museum, BC1176, BC0538, BC0548

7 Nevada and the Virginia & Truckee 203

8 From Coast to Coast

Beebe and Clegg enthusiastically embraced the lifestyle of the American West. Their reorientation from East to West began with the purchase of the *Gold Coast* in 1948. They spent summers in it under a cottonwood tree on a railroad siding in Carson City, Nevada, writing three books; *Virginia & Truckee* (1949), *U.S. West: The Saga of Wells Fargo* (1949), and *Legends of the Comstock Lode* (1950). Their transition became complete in 1950 when Beebe resigned from his newspaper job in New York City and they moved to Virginia City, Nevada.

The changes involved with their relocation also mirrored a transition in their books. While their first volumes heavily featured their own photography, the volumes to follow relied extensively on the talented photography of others, and their own photographic output diminished significantly.

They left behind their New York publishers, gradually moving their book business to Howell-North of Berkeley, California. Before the move to Nevada, there had been six railroad books. After Nevada, the total increased to twenty, and ten of them—plus several reprints—came from the printing press and bindery at Howell-North. *Steamcars to the Comstock* (1957) was the first.

Howell-North was founded in 1938 and expanded into publishing in 1956. Flora North (1917–1986), born in Siberia, was president; her husband, Morgan (1914–1978), a mining engineer, was vice president. Howell-North published other railroad books, including Jim Shaughnessy's *Delaware & Hudson*.[1] Jim and his wife enjoyed a pleasant visit to Howell-North to discuss his book as guests of Flora and Morgan in August 1967.[2]

The Norths sold the publishing house around 1980 and the new owners moved the company to San Diego and later to Los Angeles.

Kevin Bunker, who assisted Flora North when she donated Howell-North material to the California State Railroad Museum library in 1979, recalled Flora's story about the rush to finish the *The Central Pacific and the Southern Pacific Railroads*. She said, "Beebe was on hand, delaying the process by being persnickety about layout and content. They convinced him—they hoped so, at least—that time was nigh to go to press, and so he promised to 'burn the midnight oil' to get done the photo layouts and cropping he'd promised to do. He came into their publishing studio in Berkeley one afternoon with flowers—it was Flora and Morgan's anniversary—and a bottle of Tattinger champagne and told them he had made reservations in their name in S.F. for a night of swanky dining and dancing. He told them they had to get dressed and go or they'd be late.

"He promised to go right down to the studio and get to work. They dressed, left and started to enjoy the evening, which apparently ran until well after midnight. They came back to Berkeley and found the lights blazing in the studio, so they went in. Flora said she nearly had a heart attack when she saw Beebe cropping photos with an old-fashioned paper cutter, and the photos he was cropping were

---

A splendid example of Beebe's tinkering is a photo of the *Twentieth Century Limited*, with a tail sign pasted on by an artist (*The Trains We Rode*, volume 1, page 409). The image actually is a builder's photo from Pullman lot 3383, in the Smithsonian Institution Pullman negative collection, of an observation-parlor car used by the rival Pennsylvania Railroad, photographed August 27, 1906, at Pullman, Illinois. In the archives of the California State Railroad Museum, the pasted-on sign has come unglued and fallen off the railing of the car. California State Railroad Museum BCP-TWR1-P408

In 1953, Gordon Crowell traveled from west to east, photographing railroads Beebe and Clegg had not covered. These included Colorado's potato-hauling San Luis Central with a long string of refrigerator cars (below, *Age of Steam,* page 228; *Rio Grande,* page 70) and the Osage Railroad with a train of tank cars near Webb City, Oklahoma (right). Photos by Gordon Crowell

specimen originals lent by Eastman House that should have gone back intact. She told me they wound up paying Eastman House 'several thousand dollars' as a settlement, and Eastman House said they would never again lend Howell-North or Beebe any images. She also said Beebe was three sheets to the wind while wielding the cutter blade, but oh-so-cheerful while doing it because he had gotten his promised chores done," according to Bunker.[3]

Flora North once tried to influence Beebe's cover selection, but he rebuffed her, though he accepted her edits to the text. She was one of the few editors Beebe awarded such a privilege.

Beebe sometimes showed little concern for accuracy in caption writing. If it came to an inconvenient fact interfering with a dramatic image, Beebe unhesitantly sacrificed fact. An editor for Howell-North who worked with Beebe on *The Trains We Rode* confirms an oft-told story: "Beebe had provided a photo caption for a very nice 3/4 view of a station and approaching train on an Illinois Central subsidiary. The eloquent ... [Beebe caption] mentioned ... that it was such-and-such a station on such-and-such a railroad. At the edge of the photo the station name board was visible. Not only wasn't it the correct station, it wasn't even the right railroad. The editor pointed this out to Mr. Beebe. 'Well, young man, this photo contains the ambiance and pathos I wish at this particular place in the book. However, since you point this out...' And with that he took the photo to a paper cutter. WHACK! 'Now it doesn't say that, does it?'"[4]

He and Clegg maintained a brisk publishing pace. Over the six years beginning in 1960, their list of works included *San Francisco's Golden Era; When Beauty Rode the Rails; Rio Grande, Main Line of the Rockies; Great Railroad Photographs U.S.A.;* and *The Trains We Rode*. Beebe produced six alone: *Mr. Pullman's Elegant Palace Car; Twentieth Century Limited; The Central Pacific and the Southern Pacific Railroads; Overland Limited;* and *Two Trains to Remember*.

Beebe thanked a longtime friend, who had helped on many occasions, in the acknowledgments in *Overland Limited,* writing that he was "obligated to Gerald M. Best, a repository Trismegistus of the fact and folklore of American rail transport, for reading the manuscript copy and diverting the author from numerous ways of error and directing his footsteps in the highway of veracity."

Beebe and Clegg sought contributions from other photographers for their books. Gordon Crowell, a ninety-one-year-old retired General Electric executive now living in South Carolina, recalled meeting Beebe and Clegg at a book signing and, years later, at an elegant dinner at their home. "My first acquaintance with Lucius Beebe was at a book signing in a local book store in Reno in 1950. "We chatted for quite a while. I told him that I was one of the lucky few people alive who had actually ridden the Virginia & Truckee Railroad all the way up to Virginia City, which I did at age eleven in 1937, just before that branch was torn up. He was gracious, giving me a copy of *Legends of the Comstock Lode* and signing it 'for Gordon Crowell ... Practically on the scene of the crime.'"

Crowell's interest in railroading deepened while he was a student at the University of California. "I couldn't afford to buy any railroad books but I did check out *Mixed Train Daily* from the library. That was what really knocked me out, as it did so many people. My God, look at all these little short line railroads. Oh gosh, I have to do that too."

Filled with inspiration after his graduation in 1953, he spent a frugal but fruitful autumn traveling by car from Berkeley, California, to Schenectady, New York, where a new job with General Electric awaited. He photographed all the short lines he could find in his six weeks of driving, mostly through the southern states. Whenever possible, he continued this activity for the next seven years before a transfer took him to South America in 1960.

Beebe had seen Crowell's pictures in *Railroad* magazine. He wrote him in 1955, saying he and Chuck were going to put together a book called *The Age of Steam* and asked if he would consider making up some pictures for him. "I was just on a new job with GE in New York City, working long hours, commuting, etc., and didn't really have much time for photo darkroom work. However, I sent him out a box of enlargements that I'd previously put together for my own collection. He used eleven of them in *The Age of Steam*. (Beebe also used one in *Narrow Gauge in the Rockies* and two in *Rio Grande, Main Line Through the Rockies*.) So then we began our fairly frequent correspondence.

"In 1957 I took a trip from New York to Reno to visit my mother. Lucius had said, if you are in Reno, come up and have dinner with us. So that's what I did. We met at the Bucket of Blood saloon in the historic 19th century silver mining town of Virginia City for pre-dinner libations. He was at his most affable best. All I can say is, at the age of thirty-one at the time, I was not unfamiliar with alcohol but he was a past master at it. Although I tried to limit myself to about one to his three, I was feeling no great pain by the time we wobbled up the hill from C Street to the old Piper mansion, which he had purchased and restored for his home. It was absolutely gorgeous inside. He, Chuck, and I had a luxurious dinner consisting of chicken in Sauterne, mixed peas and pearl onions, sautéed tomatoes, rolls, champagne and cherries-in-whisky plus Grand Marnier liqueur served flaming over ice cream—followed by candied violet petals, coffee and after-dinner cognac. Lucius certainly knew how to eat! We had a very lovely time and they inscribed a copy of their book *Steamcars to the Comstock* and gave it to me. He and Chuck were great people.

"In 1962, when I was working for GE in Colombia, South America, he asked if I could send him some more pictures so I made up a number of enlargements for him. Three of them were in his great coffee table book, *Great Railroad Photographs U.S.A.*

"During my retirement, I put together a book for some of my godchildren explaining how I got into my railroad photo hobby. It shows pictures of all my published photos and memorabilia like one of those 1962–1963 letters from Lucius Beebe. He had told me in a prior letter that he was having problems with his bridgework ('half my face fell out,' he wrote) which required copious quantities of liquid libations to make life tolerable. I wrote him back, when I sent the pictures, saying, 'I hope your choppers have been glued back into their proper location.' He replied 'My fangs, purest vanadium annealed with the best enamel, are in place and functioning dandy even on Nevada steer meat.' I was very pleased with the photos in *Great Railroad Photographs U.S.A.* Beebe was a jovial person and a real joy to talk with."[5]

Another photographer, Jim Ehernberger of Cheyenne, Wyoming, received a call from Beebe after his photos of the Burlington branch between Sterling, Colorado, and Cheyenne appeared in the March 1955 issue of *Trains*.

"I was working a 4 p.m. to midnight shift as a crew caller at the Union Pacific, when I received the phone call," Ehernberger recalled.

"I was overwhelmed, to say the least, getting a call from a noted author. I had viewed all of the early Beebe books at our local library, and was very familiar with the name. In that era the Beebe books were the earliest photographic pictorials available. The conversation led to his request to see additional images of the Burlington train as well as an interest in Union Pacific. After this conversation, I know for a fact that I was on a cloud for a while. I was somewhat shocked."

Beebe and Clegg sent autographed copies of the books when they included Ehernberger's photos: *The Age of Steam, When Beauty Rode the Rails,* and *Rio Grande, Mainline of the Rockies*. The inscription for *Age* said: "To Jim Ehernberger, a clear track always on the Prairie Division from Lucius Beebe and Charles Clegg."

They had very little correspondence after the Rio Grande book, but were able to meet for lunch around 1964 while Ehernberger was visiting San Francisco. "At the Palace Hotel Bar, I was to meet Lucius at noon, and there was no problem identi-

Beebe titled James Ehernberger's photo in *The Age of Steam* (page 244) "Across the Great Plains." It shows eastbound Burlington mixed train no. 160 at Campstool, Wyoming, on August 14, 1954, running on the line from Cheyenne to Sterling, Colorado. The last run for this locomotive took place on August 4, 1956, two years later.

fying that person. He wore a large-sized hat (perhaps what is known as a ten-gallon type), and had high-topped boots. It seems to me his shirt was tan (heavy weight, SF can be cold), along with tan trousers. I do recall he drank Black Jack Daniels whiskey, and he was well-known at the bar, being greeted often by various customers."[6]

Beebe and Clegg maintained their friendships with railroad presidents Alfred Perlman and John W. Barriger III. Beebe told Barriger about a trip with Al and Adele (Mrs. Perlman) on the New York Central business car as far as Chicago with "much good talk and gin."[7] Barriger replied back, "I trust your archepiscopal visit was conducted on the same high level of spirituality that used to sanctify your missionary zeal when with him in Durango."[8] There were other occasions as well, including when he rode on car no. 1 from New York to Pittsburgh for the Newcomen Dinner.[9] Beebe apologized for leaving early, saying his gout foot was giving him trouble.[10]

Barriger emerged as a patron for books produced by Beebe and Clegg which showcased the work of other photographers. Beebe and Barriger began an extensive correspondence in 1951. Beebe expressed shock when Barriger left the Monon in 1952, telling Barriger that he had become "so institutionally identified with it and the middle west in recent years that it is hard to visualize you in the grime and shuttle train business of the New Haven."[11] As president of the Pittsburgh & Lake Erie from 1956 to 1964, Barriger purchased books in quantity for friends of the railroad. Robert Smith, president of the Norfolk & Western, took Beebe and Barriger slyly to task that "the N&W Railway, which is the last remaining great exponent of 'The

Age of Steam,' was not given appropriate mention in this fine volume."[12] Barriger had distributed copies of *The Age of Steam.*

Barriger's patronage also extended to the work of Howard Fogg. Starting in 1958, Fogg produced more than sixty paintings over seven years for Barriger.[13] These paintings were exhibited in Pittsburgh and Youngstown, and Beebe loaned three of his own Fogg paintings and received gracious invitations to the exhibitions.[14]

Barriger purchased 100 copies of *Mr. Pullman's Elegant Palace Car* for a San Francisco luncheon and 250 copies for Christmas distribution.[15] He continued his bulk purchases with such titles as *The Central Pacific and the Southern Pacific Railroads,* initially purchasing 300 copies but warning Beebe not to publicize the distribution in the West since western railroads might run a "temperature" about it,[16] and 375 copies of *The Overland Limited*.[17] A penny-wise Beebe billed them at full retail price plus postage and handling. Beebe charged full price to everyone, including his sister Lucia—a true Yankee charecteristic.

Great Railroad Photographs USA, published in fall 1964, was the grand finale for Beebe and Clegg's partnership with Barriger, and an extravagant tribute to the end of Barriger's tenure at the P&LE. In a letter to Barriger, Beebe described the book as "a real honker for elegance and, if present plans shape up, a fitting gesture of farewell if you are so minded."[18]

Morgan North, the publisher, wanted a by-subscription edition of 2,000 copies. Barriger agreed to buy 550 and Beebe proposed an autographed, tipped-in front page with a line drawing of the P&LE office in Pittsburgh. "It will be worth it in prestige and personal satisfaction for having done something new and that nobody else has yet done in the field of railroad books," Beebe told Barriger.[19]

Beebe followed up with more details about the book and tipped-in page. There was pressure to get the drawing to North, since Beebe and Clegg were traveling to London, and North wanted to get

Blowing off steam on the Morristown & Erie. Clegg, California State Railroad Museum, BC2842

the insert page printed and signed "as a safeguard against possible accident to either of us."[20]

Barriger helped Beebe obtain photos for the book. He contacted the New York Central and the Pennsylvania Railroad on Beebe's behalf. But in another case, he was not successful. Beebe rejected a batch of Monon photos with the statement, "I can't use freight shots, unless it is completely unavoidable in any of my book projects now in the word foundry and, if I may level with you, these pictures aren't of the exalted aesthetic status we want for *Great Railroad Photographs*."[21]

In the introduction, he and Clegg fired off a shot at David P. Morgan, the *Trains* editor, who had turned away from publishing "miserable wedges of smoke." They wrote that at Morgan's "editorial fiat, head-end action suffered a decline and panned action shots taken from parallel-moving cars, personal portraits, trackside atmosphere, and train interiors became the preoccupation of photographers who valued his favor."[22]

Morgan's review called the book "imperfect but nonetheless welcome," and noted that the introduction "modestly omits" credit to Beebe and Clegg for preserving "so much of this priceless illustration for us and our descendants."[23]

Beebe and Clegg's commercial success drew criticism from Charles E. Fisher (1889–1972), the president of the Railway & Locomotive Historical Society. Beebe fired back in a letter to Morgan, "That fine old bundle of black bombazine petulance ... has been sitting around for years now gnashing his store teeth at lapses in traction force statistics in other people's books who at least have the energy ... and, if I may be pardoned the pretentiousness, [the] dedication to contribute something to the bibliography of rail transport."[24]

Beebe and Clegg's last work was the magnificent two-volume *The Trains We Rode,* a pictorial record of the best and most interesting passenger trains of the U.S. and Canada. Clegg finished the second volume after Beebe's death. Another book, not about railroads, also was released after Beebe's death: *The Big Spenders.*[25]

Two posthumous collections of Beebe's writings honored him; *The Lucius Beebe Reader* (1967), compiled by Clegg with Duncan Emrich, and *The Provocative Pen of Lucius Beebe, Esq.* (1966), a collection of *San Francisco Chronicle* columns.

It was a good run, with a long succession of railroad books. While over too early, the Beebe and Clegg journey showed the way and injected life and hope into railroad publishing.

Notes

1. Jim Shaughnessy, *Delaware & Hudson: The History of an Important Railroad Whose Antecedent Was a Canal Network to Transport Coal* (Berkeley, Calif.: Howell-North Books), 1967.
2. Interview with Shaughnessy, Troy, New York, March 12, 2017.
3. Kevin Bunker to John Gruber, Feb. 28, 2017.
4. Harry Aitken, interview with Gruber, Western Railroad Museum, n.d.
5. Interview with Gordon Crowell, updated March 17, 2017.
6. Ehernberger, accounts and experiences, email to Gruber, June 22, 2017.
7. Beebe to Barriger, March 6, 1963, John W. Barriger III Railroad Library, St. Louis.
8. Barriger to Beebe, March 16, 1963. Barriger Library.
9. Perlman to Beebe, May 27, 1963, Barriger Library.
10. Beebe to Barriger, June 7, 1963, Barriger Library.
11. Beebe to Barriger, Dec. 22, 1952, Barriger Library.
12. Barriger to Beebe, Jan. 29, 1958, Barriger Library.
13. Jerry W. Jordak, "Postcards from the Pittsburgh & Lake Erie," *Railroad Heritage* 2017: 1 (Madison, Wis.: Center for Railroad Photography & Art), 36-45.
14. Barriger to Beebe, Dec. 5, 1958, Barriger Library.
15. Barriger to Beebe, Oct. 24, 1961, Barriger Library.
16. Barriger to Beebe, April 13, 1963, Barriger Library.
17. Beebe to Barriger, Feb. 26, 1964, Barriger Library.
18. Beebe to Barriger, April 20, 1963, Barriger Library.
19. Beebe to Barriger, Nov. 26, 1963, Barriger Library.
20. Beebe to Barriger, March 10, 1964, Barriger Library.
21. Beebe to Barriger, undated, received Feb. 7, 1964, Barriger Library.
22. Beebe and Clegg, *Great Railroad Photographs,* Introduction, 10.
23. Morgan, "Of Books and Trains," *Trains,* Dec. 1949, 51.
24. Beebe to Morgan, Dec. 7, 1962, Kalmbach Library.
25. Lucius Beebe, *The Big Spenders: the Epic Story of the Rich Rich, the Grandees of America and the Magnificoes, and How They Spent Their Fortunes* (Garden City, N.Y.: Doubleday, 1966).

9 Their Photographic Legacy

At a time when railroad books were almost unknown, it took a celebrity writer of the stature of Lucius M. Beebe to transform the seemingly prosaic subject of railroads into books that beguiled the public. His first railroad book, *High Iron* (1938), was a success which won a widespread audience for railroad photography and brought more fame for Beebe.

Charles M. Clegg, Jr., joined him in 1941. Together they published about thirty more books and captured thousands of pictures of railroads, of which only a relative few have been published. While the decades have been kind to their books, many of which are now collector's items, knowledge of their photographic archive was limited mostly to their published images.

It is time to reconsider Beebe and Clegg's pictures and their distinctive styles of photography, and to put them into newer contexts such as the thematic groups shown and discussed here. This retrospective is made possible by the generous gift from Clegg's sister, Ann Clegg Holloway and

her husband, John Ennis Holloway, of Beebe and Clegg's surviving photographs and papers to the California State Railroad Museum Library.

In the foreword to *Highliners: A Railroad Album* (1940), Beebe noted that not all photographs "abide by the most rigid classic requirements. Some have been taken from other than the three-quarters head-on angle required by exacting collectors of action shots." Railroad photographers need "sterner stuff," he wrote in the first issue of *Trains,* November 1940.

A Midland Terminal train, with empty ore cars and locomotives on the front and back, climbs a steep grade near Midland, Colorado, a station between Divide and Cripple Creek. The railroad operated on a remaining section of the Colorado Midland between Colorado Springs and Divide, where its rails turn north to Victor and Cripple Creek. Beebe, California State Railroad Museum, BC2393

Two Consolidation locomotives of the Midland Terminal hike a train of empty ore cars up a steep four percent grade at Midland, Colorado. The train is headed for mines at Victor and Cripple Creek. Clegg, *MTD*, page 230. California State Railroad Museum, BC2374

Beebe's choice of photographic angles expanded beyond the three-quarters "wedge" perspective after he partnered with Clegg. Classically-trained Clegg's pictorial-school ideas emphasized beauty, a contrast to Beebe's insistence on drama. Beebe's silhouette of a train on the Denver & Salt Lake climbing the front range near Denver *(Highball,* page 203, and similar to the Clegg view shown on page 78 of this volume) suggests the stylistic transformation of his work.

The four railroad photo books published between 1938 and 1945 established Beebe and Clegg as experts in their field. In "Railroads Are American" in *American Photography,* October 1947, Beebe admitted that *Mixed Train Daily* had departed from previous standards, and used the plural "we" to recognize Clegg's pictorial influence. "We aimed to include backgrounds and atmospheric incidentals which would suggest the countryside in which each little railroad had its being, and action shots in the depots and yards of remote farlands which would depict its social and economic function," he said.[1]

While Beebe usually espoused a straightforward, wedge-of-pie perspective, he encouraged the creative, cutting-edge styles of other photographers. The most dramatic example is the top billing for Richard Steinheimer (1929–2011), then 34, in *The Central Pacific and the Southern Pacific Railroads, With 121 photos by Richard Steinheimer* (Howell-North, 1963).

Other books showcased the work of James Shaughnessy, Jim Gallagher (1920–2002), and Phil Hastings (1925–1987), winners of the Railway & Locomotive Historical Society's photography award; Robert Hale (1912–1992), known for "panned" photographs of trains in motion; Donald Duke (1929–2010), publisher of Golden West Books; and more. The acknowledgments in their books are a who's who of contemporary photographers.

Their flair for promotion meant that some of their books received more attention than competing projects, such as Simpson Kalisher's *Railroad*

Men (1961). Beebe inquired about using Kalisher's photos in a Beebe-Clegg book, but Kalisher charged a fee and Beebe did not want to pay it.[2]

Beebe contributed essays to others' books, like those of Arthur D. Dubin (1923–2011). Dubin was an important photograph collector, architect, and fellow railroad historian. Beebe wrote the foreword to Dubin's *Some Classic Trains* (Kalmbach, 1964), offering more perspectives on photography, noting that by the late 1930s railroad photography books had become a profitable venture. "You must know that I appreciate that your [passenger] car [photo] collection is your life's blood and that sharing it with anyone else is a remarkable tribute to your good heart," Beebe wrote to Dubin in 1961.

Dubin and David P. Morgan, editor of *Trains,* offered Beebe an opportunity to review proofs of Dubin's manuscript for *Trains* (August 1962) about the *Twentieth Century Limited,* and Beebe incorporated Dubin's material in his *Twentieth Century, the Greatest Train in the World* (Howell-North, 1962).

Beebe and Clegg had an uncanny ability to document railroads that are now national treasurers, such as the East Broad Top, Cumbres & Toltec Scenic, and Durango & Silverton, plus Amtrak's *California Zephyr* route through Colorado. Their favorite, the Virginia & Truckee, survives as a tourist hauler on a partially rebuilt section between Virginia City and Carson City.

Beebe and Clegg's cross-country travel in their private railroad cars added to their allure. Their first car, the *Gold Coast,* is now on permanent display at the California State Railroad Museum, and it played host to then-Governor Ronald Reagan and his wife Nancy for a dinner that precipitated the founding of the museum.

The Nevada Writers Hall of Fame, an annual honor of the University of Nevada, Reno, libraries, recognized Beebe,[3] as proposed by Andria Daley, a Beebe specialist. In his entry, it says of him, "A highly civilized non-conformist, Beebe thought of himself as a Renaissance Man and a true snob and was recognized as a legend in his own lifetime." The entry concludes with Beebe's own statement, "All I want is the best of everything and there's so very little of that."

Generations of railroad enthusiasts can testify to their influence. When author Gruber was in his early teens, his parents routinely presented him with railroad books. Beebe and Clegg's were among his favorites. He was never one to seek out autographs, but on a family trip to Virginia City in 1953, they stopped at the *Territorial Enterprise* office and Gruber asked Beebe to sign his copy of *Mixed Train Daily*. Beebe obliged. Amongst the hundreds of books in Gruber's collection, he treasures it especially. Author Ryan's first exposure to railroad photography books was through a shelf-worn collection of Beebe and Clegg books at his local library.

They have not been forgotten. At a presentation for the Center for Railroad Photography & Art in 2016, about eighty percent of the audience recognized their names and expressed familiarity with their work.

Beebe and Clegg were the right people at the right time to bring the heroism, charm, and history of railroading to the public. Their photography and their writing demonstrated the importance of railroading in community life and contributed to America's historical legacy. Together Beebe and Clegg created more than thirty books on railroading and Western Americana. Their legacy has grown larger than the publications they produced, as they demonstrated that the railroad serves the nation as an icon of American experience.

Notes

1. Beebe, "Railroads Are American," *American Photography,* Oct. 1947.
2. Simpson Kalisher, *Railroad Men: A Book of Photographs and Collected Stories* (New York: Clarke & Way, 1961); and Kalisher to Beebe, Feb., 13, 1962, CSRM library.
3. Nevada Writers Hall of Fame, 1992, http://guides.library.unr.edu/nvwriters-hall-of-fame/beebe-1992.

Beebeography

By Martin K. O'Toole, *an enthusiastic collector of Beebe materials who lists books in his library here*

1921: *Fallen Stars* (autographed) *Fallen stars,* by Lucius Beebe. Boston. The Cornhill Publishing Company 1921, 7 p. l., 31 p. 20 cm

1924: *Corydon and Other Poems,* by Lucius Beebe. Boston, B. J. Brimmer Company, 1924. 64 p. 24 cm.

1925: *Francois Villon Certain Aspects,* by Lucius Beebe. Cambridge, Mass., Samuel Marcus Press, 1925. 30 p. Limited to fifty copies.

1927: *Edwin Arlington Robinson and the Arthurian legend,* by Lucius Beebe. Cambridge, Mass., Samuel Marcus Press, 30 p., 1 l. 24 cm First printing, September 1927, limited to 100 numbered copies. Second edition in November 1927.

1928: *Aspects of the Poetry of Edwin Arlington Robinson* (#225 of a limited edition of 225). Cambridge, Mass., Privately printed, 1928.

1931: *A Bibliography of the Writings of Edwin Arlington Robinson,* by Lucius Beebe and Robert J. Bulkley, Jr. (Limited edition of 300 copies). Cambridge, Mass., The Dunster House Bookshop, 1931. 59 p., 1 l. 21 cm.

1934: *People on Parade,* by Jerome Zerbe (1904-88); with an introduction by Lucius Beebe. New York, D. Kemp, 1934. 105 p. illus. 28 cm

1935: *Boston and the Boston Legend,* by Lucius Beebe, illustrations by E. H. Suydam. New York, London, D. Appleton-Century Company, Incorporated, 1935. xv, 372 p. col. front., illus., plates. 24 cm.

1938: *High Iron: A Book of Trains,* by Lucius Beebe. New York, London, D. Appleton-Century Company, 1938. xiii, 225, [1] p. illus., plates. 29 cm.

1940: *Highliners: A Railroad Album,* by Lucius Beebe. New York, London, D. Appleton-Century Company incorporated, 1940. xvi, [2] p. incl. front., 103 pl. 21 x 29 cm.

1941: *Trains in Transition,* by Lucius Beebe. New York, London, D. Appleton-Century Company, Incorporated, 1941. xiii, 210 p. incl. front., illus. 29 x 22 cm.

1943: *Snoot if You Must,* by Lucius Beebe; drawings by Rea Irvin. New York, London, D. Appleton-Century Company, Incorporated, 1943. 296 p. illus. 21 cm.

1945: *Highball: A Pageant of Trains,* by Lucius Beebe. New York, London, D. Appleton-Century Company, Incorporated [1945] xiii, 223, [2] p. incl. front., illus. 29 cm.

1946: *The Narrow Gauge Railroads of Colorado,* by Lucius Beebe. Boston, Railway & Locomotive Historical Society, August, 1946. 47 p. illus. 15.5 x 23 cm.

1946: *The Stork Club Bar Book,* by Lucius Beebe. New York, Toronto, Rinehart & Company, inc., 1946, undated reprint. xiii p., 1 l., 17-136 p. 21 cm.

1947: *Mixed Train Daily: A Book of Shortline Railroads,* by Lucius Beebe with photographs by C. M. Clegg, Jr., and the author and six original oil paintings by Howard Fogg. 1st ed. New York, Dutton, 1947. xiii, 367 p. illus. (some color), maps. 29 cm.

1948: *Dreadful California,* Edited work by Helper, Hinton Rowan, 1829-1909. Dreadful California, being a true and scandalous account of the barbarous civilization, licentious morals, crude manners and depravities, inclement climate and niggling resources, together with various other offensive and calamitous details of life in the Golden State, ed. by Lucius Beebe and Charles Clegg. Illus. by James Alexander. Indianapolis, Bobbs-Merrill [1948] 162 p. illus. 21 cm.

1949: *U.S. West: The Saga of Wells Fargo,* by Lucius Beebe and Charles Clegg. [1st ed.] New York, E.P. Dutton, 1949. 320 p. illus., ports., maps. 27 cm.

1949: *Virginia & Truckee; a story of Virginia City and Comstock times,* by Lucius Beebe and Charles Clegg; decorations by E. S. Hammack, maps and lettering by Frederic Shaw. [1st ed.] Oakland, Calif., G. H. Hardy, 1949. 58 [5] p. illus., ports., maps. 24 cm.

1950: *The Legends of the Comstock Lode,* by Lucius Beebe and Charles Clegg. Decorations by E. S. Hammack. Oakland, Calif., G. H. Hardy, 1950. 79 p. illus., ports., map. 23 cm.

1951: *Cable Car Carnival,* by Lucius Beebe and Charles Clegg. Decorations by E. S. Hammack. [1st ed.] Oakland, Calif., G. H. Hardy, 1951. 130 p. illus., ports., map. 29 cm.

1952: *Hear The Train Blow: A pictorial epic of America in the railroad age,* by Lucius Beebe and Charles Clegg. With 10 original drawings by E. S. Hammack and 860 illus. New York, Grosset & Dunlap, 1952. 407 p. illus., ports. 29 cm.

1954: *Comstock Commotion: The Story of the Territorial Enterprise and Virginia City News.* Stanford, Stanford University Press, 1954. 129 p. illus., ports. 25 cm.

1955: *The American West: The Pictorial Epic of a Continent,* by Lucius Beebe and Charles Clegg. With title page in color by E. S. Hammack and more than 1,000 illus. [1st ed.] New York, Dutton, 1955. 511 p. illus., ports., map. 29 cm.

1957: *The Age of Steam: A Classic Album of American Railroading,* by Lucius Beebe and Charles Clegg. New York, Rinehart [1957] 304 p. illus. 29 cm.

1957: *Steam Cars to the Comstock: The Virginia & Truckee Railroad, the Carson & Colorado Railroad:* their story in picture and prose, by Lucius Beebe and Charles Clegg. Berkeley, Calif., Howell-North Books, 1957. 74 p. illus. 29 cm.

1958: *Narrow Gauge in the Rockies,* by Lucius Beebe and Charles Clegg. Berkeley, Calif., Howell-North Books, 1958. 224 p. illus. (part color) maps (1 on lining papers) diagrams., facsimiles., 29 cm.

1959: *Mansions on Rails: The Folklore of the Private Railroad Car,* by Lucius Beebe. Berkeley, Calif., Howell-North Books, 1959. 382 p. illus. (part color) plans. 28 cm.

1960: *San Francisco's Golden Era: A picture story of San Francisco before the fire,* by Lucius Beebe and Charles Clegg. Berkeley, Calif., Howell-North Books, 1960. 255 p. illus. 29 cm.

1961: *Mr. Pullman's Elegant Palace Car:* the railway carriage that established a new dimension of luxury and entered the national lexicon as a symbol of splendor, by Lucius Beebe. Garden City, N.Y., Doubleday, 1961. 574 p. illus. ports. 29 cm.

1962: *When Beauty Rode the Rails: An album of Railroad Yesterdays,* by Lucius Beebe and Charles Clegg. [1st ed.] Garden City, N.Y., Doubleday [1962]. 222 p. illus. 29 cm.

1962: *Rio Grande: Mainline of the Rockies,* by Lucius Beebe and Charles Clegg. Berkeley, Calif., Howell-North, 1962. 380 p. illus. (part color) maps. 29 cm.

1962: *Rio Grande: Mainline of the Rockies,* by Lucius Beebe and Charles Clegg. Berkeley, Calif., Howell-North, 1962. Timberline Limited Edition. Signed by both authors and in a slip case. Mylar cover. 1250 copy edition. Map in rear pocket. 380 p. illus. (part color) maps. 29 cm.

1962: *Twentieth Century: The Greatest Train in the World,* by Lucius Beebe. Berkeley, Calif., Howell-North Books, 1962. 180 p. illus. 29 cm.

1963: *The Overland Limited,* by Lucius Beebe. Berkeley, Calif., Howell-North Books, 1963. 157 p. illus. (part color) ports., map, facsimiles. 29 cm.

1963: *The Central Pacific and the Southern Pacific Railroads, With 121 photos by Richard Steinheimer,* by Lucius Beebe. Berkeley, Calif., Howell-North, 1963. 631 p. illus. 29 cm.

1964: *Great Railroad Photographs, U.S.A.,* (Limited to 2,000 copies) by Lucius Beebe and Charles Clegg. Berkeley, Calif., Howell-North Books, 1964. 243 p. illus. (part color) ports. 32 cm.

1965: *Two Trains to Remember: The New England Limited, The Air Line Limited,* by Lucius Beebe. [Virginia City? Nev.] 1965. 54 p. illus. (part color) 24 cm.

1965: *The Trains We Rode,* Volume 1, by Lucius Beebe and Charles Clegg. Berkeley, Calif., Howell-North Books, 1965. 2 v. illus. (part color) 29 cm.

1966: *The Trains We Rode,* Volume 2, by Lucius Beebe and Charles Clegg. Berkeley, Calif., Howell-North Books, 1966. 2 v. illus. (part color) 29 cm.

1966: *The Big Spenders,* by Lucius Beebe. [1st ed.] Garden City, N.Y., Doubleday, 1966. xxiv, 404 p. illus., ports. 24 cm.

1966: *The Provocative Pen of Lucius Beebe, Esq.* San Francisco, Chronicle Pub. Co. [1966] xv, 275 p. 24 cm.

1967: *The Lucius Beebe Reader.* Edited by Charles Clegg and Duncan Emrich. [1st ed.] Garden City, N.Y., Doubleday, 1967. 398 p. 24 cm.

Also see Nevada Writers Hall of Fame, 1992, http://guides.library.unr.edu/nvwriters-hall-of-fame/beebe-1992

Index

A
Abraham Lincoln **60**, 61
Alamosa, Colo. **80**, 81, 154, 155, 164
Age of Steam 28, 207, 208, 210
Allston, Mass. 56, 57
Alton **60**
Amador Central 146, **147**
American Locomotive Co. 18
American Mercury 42, 43
American Photography 214, 215
Anderson, Harold L. 166
Andreasen, Earl and Mary 23
Appleton-Century Co. 39, 40, 55
Arnold Constable & Co. 14
Arzrouni, Jerry 59
Atchison, Topeka & Santa Fe 22, **49**, **54**, 55, **88**, **89**, **90**, **91**, 94
Atlantic & Western Railway **114**
Aztec, N. Mex. 164

B
Baker, Ore. 176, 178
Baker, Mose 151
Baltimore & Ohio **48**
Barriger, John W. III 24, 25, 155, 209, 210
Barriger, John W. IV (Jack) 155
Barriger, Stanley 155
Bates, Ore. 156
Best-dressed men 39
Beebe, Eleanor Harriett Merrick 36
Beebe, Junius 36, 39
Beebe, Junius Merrick 36
Beebe, Junius Oliver 36
Beebe Library 36
Begger, Catherine 27
Bellefonte Central **126**
Berkeley, Calif. 23, **92**, 205, 207
Berkshire School, Sheffield, Mass. 36
Best, Gerald M. 207
Bieber, Calif. 53
Boehner, John 4
Borie, Wyo. 4, **84**
Boston, Mass 36, 41, 65
Boston & Albany 36, 55, **56**
Boston and the Boston Legend 39, 55
Boston Evening Transcript 38
Boston & Maine 57, **66**
Boston Telegram 38
Bowden Railway **122**
Brennan, James A. **115**, 188
Bristol, Horace 47
Brown Palace Hotel 9
Brown, Willie 21
Bucket of Blood saloon 208
Budd, John M. 53
Buffalo Creek & Gauley **115**
Bunker, Kevin 205, 207
Burns, Roy 25

C
Cable Car Carnival 23
Caen, Herb 11, 26
Café Society 13, 25, 38, 43, 55
Cajon Pass **94**
California State Railroad Museum Library 9, 213
California Zephyr 26, 53, 215
Cameras, their 33
Camino, Placerville & Lake Tahoe 147, **148**, **149**
Camp, Alfred P. 154, **166**
Campbell, Clair **166**
Carolina Blues 15
Carracas, Colo. 162, **163**
Carson City, Nev. 9, 18, 159, 192, 193, 194, **196**, 197, 198, 199, 205
Carson & Colorado 159, 182
Carson & Colorado Railway (volunteer) 159, 182
Center for Railroad Photography & Art 215
Central City (Colo.)
Opera 9, 27, 38
Central of Geogia 31, 107, **117**
Central Pacific and the Southern Pacific, The 205, 207
Cerf, Bennett 15
Chesapeake & Ohio 72, 115, 130
Cheyenne, Wyo. 4, 84, 85, 208, 209
Chicago, Milwaukee, St. Paul & Pacific 62, **63**, 136
Chicago, Rock Island & Pacific 41, 47, 76
Chicago, Ill. 22, 41, 42, 62, **63**, **64**, **65**
Chicago, Burlington & Quincy 60, **209**
Chicago & North Western 63
Chicago & Western Indiana 70
Cholly Knickerbocker, see: Paul, Maury
City of Los Angeles 42, 55, 100
City of San Francisco **37**, **92**
Clegg, Ann, see: Holloway, Ann Clegg
Clegg, Charles M., Sr. 14
Clegg, Myles S. 27
Clegg, Ruth Standish 14, 27
Cleveland, Ohio 11, 40
Colletti, Edward S. 26
Colorado Railroad Museum 104, 155, 160
Colorado & South Eastern **102**, **103**
Colorado & Southern **48**, **78**
Columbus & Greenville **110**
Colou, Art 25
Commodore Vanderbilt **65**
Connors, Dan 20

Copper Range Railroad 103, **136**, **137**
Cornish, George A. 20
Corydon and Other Poems 27
Costa, Joseph 18
Coster, Gordon 47
Gordon Crowell 206, 207, 208
Crowell-Spencer Lumber Co. **112**
Cowley, Malcolm 101
Crum, John H. 154
Crusader **64**

D
Daley, Andria 20, 23, 215, 224
Danville & Western **138**
Dardanelle & Russellville **138**, **139**
Daylight locomotive **86**
DeKalb & Western **51**
Delano, Jack 47
Delaware, Lackawanna & Western 47, **70**
Delaware & Hudson [railroad] 67
Delaware & Hudson [book] 205
Denver & Rio Grande Western 7, 13, 17, **51**, 81, **82**, **83**, 153, 154, 155, **160**, **161**, 162, **163**, 164, **165**, 169, **170**, **171**
Denver & Salt Lake 214
Dettinger, Alma 18
Dickersohn, Theodore von 153, 155
Dmitri, Ivan 46, 50
Dolores, Colo. 154, **168**, 169, **172**
Donovan, Frank P., Jr. 104
Douglas, Nev. 192
Dubin, Arthur D. 215
Duke, Donald 214
Dupont, Alfred F. 109
Durango, Colo. 154, 155, **160**, 162, **163**, 164, 166, 171, 209
Durango & Silverton Narrow Gauge Railroad 153, 154, 160, 215
Dutton, E. P. & Co. 103

E
East Broad Top 104, 153, 156, 159, **186**, **187**, 215
East Tennessee & Western North Carolina 153, 156, **188**, **189**, **190**, **191**
Ehernberger, Jim 208, 209
Elizabethton, Tenn. 156, **188**
Emrich, Duncan 26, **211**
Erie Railroad 57, **67**
Erie Railroad Magazine 103
Esquire 13
Exposition Flyer **81**

F
Farmington, N.Mex. 164
Farm Security Administration 47, 198
Ferdinand 48
Fields, W. C. 39
Fisher, Charles E. 211

Florence & Cripple Creek 171
Fogg, Howard 100, 210
Fontes, Andrew 25
Ford Times 13
Fortune 47
Frankfort & Cincinnati 48, **132**, **133**
French, Windsor 26
Fryk, Arnold "Bill" **195**

G
Gainesville Midland **120**, **121**
Gallagher, Jim 214
Galloping Goose 154, **172**, **173**
Garfinckel's Department Store 14
Georgia & Florida 107
Georgia Northern 18, 31, **119**
Gibbs, Wolcott 38, 40
Gibson, Owen V. **34**, **35**
Gilt Edge Limited **65**
Gold Coast (railroad car) 9, 18, 19, **31**, 53, 193, 198, 205, 215
Golden Peak (railroad car) 19
Golden Spike National Historic Site 35
Goldfield, Nev. 159
Gotham DeLuxe 15
Gourmet 13
Graflex camera **5**, 17, **32**, 33, 40
Grand Trunk Western **62**
Graves, Roy D. 198
Great Northern **58**
Great Railroad Photographs U.S.A. 24, 28, 207, 208, 210
Graebing, Clayton W. 154, 166
Green Diamond **61**
Green Light 155, 159
Gruber, John 28, 30, 43, 59, 105, 159, 199, 211, 215, **224**
Guffey, Paulette 13
Gulf, Mobile & Ohio 103, **112**

H
Hale, L. H. 154, 166
Hale, Robert 24, 214
Hammack, E. S. **19**
Hanley, Robert T. 19
Hardy, Grahame H. 28, 195
Harper's Weekly 13
Hart, James 22
Harvard University 36, 38
Harvey, Byron 22
Haskell, Elizabeth 39, 40
Haskell, William E., Jr. 39
Hastings, Phil 24, 214
Henry, Robert Selph 11
Highball, A Pageant of Trains 55, 57
Hines, Henry 154
Hiawatha 62, **63**
High Iron: A Book of Trains 40, 55, **219**
Highliners: A Railroad Album 37, 57, 213

Hillsborough, Calif. 23, **24**, 25, 27
Hine, Lewis 47
Hoffman, Bernard 47
Holbrook, Stewart 59
Holiday 13, 20, 53, 155
Holloway, Ann Clegg **8**, **9**, **12** 13, 18, 27, **44**, **45**, 212
Holloway, Charles 18
Holloway, John "Jack" 9, 18, 27
Holloway, Jay 18
Holloway, Peter 9, 18, 27
Holloway, Colo. 78
Hooppole, Yorktown & Tampico **134**, **135**
Hoover, J. Edgar 11, **13**, 100
Howell-North Books 23, 26, 205, 207
Hubbard, Freeman 40, 55

I
Illinois Central **51**, **61**, 207
Illman, John 198
Illustrated London News 21

J
Jeffers, William M. 42
Jenkisson, John 198
Jersey Central **68**
Jim Crow cars 100, **101**, **106**, 107
Johnson City, Tenn. 156, 194, 196
Jones, Casey 96, **97**, 103

K
Kalisher, Simpson 214
Kansas City, Mo. **60**, 61
Kansas City Southern 78, **79**
Kentucky Railway Museum 132
Kneiss, Gilbert H. **25**, 52, 53

L
Lake Forest, Ill. 62, **63**
Laramie, Wyo. 4, **85**, 142
Laramie, North Park & Western **142**, **143**
Laube, Winfield 154
Laurentian **67**
Laws, Calif. 159, **180**, **182**
Lehigh & New England **69**
"*Life* Goes to a Party" 8, 18, **44**, **45**, 100
Life magazine 8, 18, 41, 45, 47, 50, 101, 198
Live Oak, Perry & Gulf **32**, 33, **51**
Lizard Head Pass, Colo. 155, 166, **167**, **173**
Look 47
Lootens, J. Ghislain 17, 47, 50
Louisville & Nashville 74, **75**
Louisville, New Albany & Corydon **129**
Louisville & Wadley 104, 107
Lucius Beebe Reader 26, 211

M
Madison Hotel 13, 20, 38, **42**

High Iron, Beebe's first railroad book, published in 1938, inspired the cover of this book. Holloway collection

Manchester & Oneida 103, **131**
Mancos, Colo. **174**
Marianna & Blountstown **109**
Marranzino, Pasquale "Pocky" 154, 155, **166**, **167**
Marshall, Sally Holloway 18
Maryland & Pennsylvania Railroad **8**, 9, 18, **44**, **45**, 103
McEwen, Oreg. 179
McKeen Motor Car **196**, 197
McKeever, Mich. 136
McLean, Evalyn Walsh 11, 13, 38
McLean, Ned 13
Medalist camera **5**, 17, 33, **154**, 177
Meem, Ann Carol 13
Merchants Express 70
Mercury 64, **65**
Merrick, John Mudge 36
Merrilees, Andrew 100
Mexican Northern Railway & Mining Co. 36
Mid-Continent Railway Historical Society 104, 136
Midland Terminal **213**, 214
Midland Valley **51**, **110**
Mississippi & Alabama **112**
Mills, Darius Ogden 19, 195
Milwaukee Road, see Chicago, Milwaukee, St. Paul & Pacific
Minden, Nev. 192
Mississippi & Alabama **113**
Missouri-Kansas-Texas **76**
Mixed Train Daily 5, 9, 17, 18, 23, 28, 33, 59, 98, 100, 103, 104, 105, 153, 156, 160, 198, 199, 200, 207, 214, 215

Index 219

Lucius Beebe and Dave Chasen sit with T-Bone Towser I in Virginia City in front of the *Territorial Enterprise* office in 1958. Chasen, a comedian, and his wife, Maude, operated the popular Chasen's, a restaurant near Beverly Hills, California, that served the Hollywood elite. Beebe and Clegg went there frequently when they were in the area. Clegg, Michael McCreary collection

Model Builder 104
Monon 210
Morehead & North Fork **130**
Morgan, David P. 24, 25, 40, 47, 104, 210, 211, 215
Morgan, Willard 18
Morley, Colo. **54**, 55
Morley, Jim 198
Morristown & Erie Railroad 140, **141**, **210**
Mowbray, Cathlyn Hammes 198
Mr. Pullman's Elegant Palace Car 207, 210
Museum of Science and Industry 61

N
Narrow Gauge Kingdom 160
National Historic Landmark 104, 156, 160, 175
National Register of Historic Places 197
Navy Reserve 14

Nevada Copper Belt **194**, 198
Nevada State Railroad Museum 197
Nevada Writers Hall of Fame 215
Newhall, Scott 27
Newsweek 55
New York Central 17, **46**, 65, **153**, **209**, 210
New York Herald Tribune 13, 38, 43, 55, 59, 155, 199
New York, New Haven & Hartford 39, **65**, 209
New York Times 21, 50, 59, 104
Norfolk & Western 209
North, Flora 205, 207
North, Morgan 205
North, Sterling 101
Northern Pacific 13

O
Omaha, Neb. 42, 61, 197

Oneida, Tenn. 72, **73**
Ophir, Colo. 155, **168**, **169**
Osage Railroad **206**
O'Sheel, Patrick 18
Overland Limited [book] 207, 210
Overland Limited [train] 62, **63**, 85
Overton, Richard 103

P
Pacific Coast Chapter, R&LHS 19, 53
Pacific Limited **94**
Palace Hotel **16**, 208
Palmer, Stanley G. 198
Parker, Dorothy 57
Paul, Maury 43
Peck, C. B. 18
Pennoyer, Sheldon 100
Pennsylvania Railroad **68**, **70**, **71**, 187
Pellet, Elizabeth 155, 166, **167**
People on Parade 39
Perlman, Alfred E. 17, 18, 25, 28, 153, 154, 155, **166**, 209
Phillips, Jay C. 154
Phyfe, Hal 13
Piney River & Paint Creek 36
Pioneer Zephyr **60**, 61
Piper family 20
Piper, John, House 11, 20, **27**, 28, **29**, 208
Piper's Opera House 20
Pittsburgh & Lake Erie 24, 209, 210
Prescott & Northwestern **123**
Promontory, Utah 35
Provines, June 41
Pyle, Ernie 39

Q
Quist, Carl E. 154

R
Railroad magazine 55
Railroad fans 17, 39
Railtown 1897 151
Railway & Locomotive Historical Society 19, 41, 53, 100, 211, 214
Rapp, Frank **26**, 27
Raritan River **48**, **127**
Rasmussen, Frank 154
Raton, N.Mex. **89**, **90**, **91**
Raton Pass 54, 55, **89**, **90**, **91**
Reading **51**, 64
Reed, William 153, 154
Reid, Helen 195
Reid, Ogden 39
Reno Gazette-Journal 199
Reynolds, Horace 50, 104
Richardson, Robert W. 104, 155
Richmond, Fredericksburg & Potomac **73**
Rico, Colo. 155, 166, 168, 172, **173**
Ridgway, Colo. 154, 155

Rio Grande, Main Line of the Rockies 207, 208
Rio Grande Southern 17, 153, 154, **157, 158**, 159, **166, 167, 168, 169, 170, 171, 172, 173, 174**
Robertson, Archie 100, 156
Robinson, Elmer E. 23
Rock Island, see: Chicago, Rock Island & Pacific
Rocket 76
Rockwood, Colo. 160
Rockwood, Lucia Beebe 36
Rocky Ford, Ga. **116**, 117
Rocky Mountain News 30, 154
Rolls-Royce 20, 23, **24**, 28, **29**
Rothstein, Arthur 198
Roxbury School, Cheshire, Conn. 36
Russell, Andrew J. 35
Russell, Governor Charles 20

S
Saillard, Louis 100, 113
Sampson, Gordon A. 192, 195, 198
Sandersville Railroad **101**
San Francisco, Calif. 15, 16, 23, 25, 38, 53, 86, 202, 208
San Francisco Chronicle 11, 23, 26, 27, 211
San Francisco's Golden Era 207
San Juan 154, 155, **162, 163**
San Luis Central **206**
San Luis Valley Southern 49, 142, **143, 144, 145**
Santa Fe, see: Atchison, Topeka & Santa Fe
Sawyer, Arthur 36
Sazerac Saloon 23
Schaal, Eric 47
Sharon, William 159
Shaughnessy, Jim 24, 205, 214
Shelter, Roy 23
Sherman Hill, Wyo. 4
Sierra Railroad **150, 151**
Slow Train to Yesterday 100
Smith, Claude 154
Smith, Mike S. 154
Smith, Robert 209
Smoky Mountain **118**
Snoot If You Must 15, 57
Some Classic Trains 215
Southern Railway 47, 72, **73**
Southern Pacific 18, 35, 37, 47, **59**, 86, 92, **93, 95**,
  dining car department 19, 21
  narrow gauge 5, 153, 159, **180, 181, 182, 183, 184, 185**
Sparks, Nev. 19, 41, **58**, 92, 198
Sporer, Andrew W. 154
Standish, Granville Searcy 14
Starkville, Colo. **88**
Steamcars to the Comstock 23, 198, 205, 208

Steichen, Edward 47
Steinheimer, Richard 24, 214
Stephens, Yvone Jean 42
Sterling, Colo. 208, 209
Stillwater, Okla. **15**
St. Johnsbury & Lake Champlain 47, **124, 125**
St. Louis, Mo. 15, 42, **60**, 61
St. Louis-San Francisco 78
St. Louis Union Station 42, **60**, 61
St. Marks, Southboro, Mass. 36
Sumpter Valley 153, 156, **176, 177, 178, 179**
Sunset Limited 92
Sylvania Central 107, **116**, 117

T
Tallulah Falls **122**
T-Bone Towser I, II 18, 23, 28, **220**
Telluride, Colo. 154, 155, 172, **175**
Territorial Enterprise 11, 20, 21, **22**, 215
Texas & Pacific **48**
Thayer, Mary Van Rensselaer 99, 100
The Trains We Rode 26, 28, 205, 207, 211
"This New York" 15
This Week 13
"This Wild West" 23
Thomas, Clark I. 154
Thomas, George 154
Time 155
Tonopah & Goldfield, 198, **202**, 203
Tonopah Junction, Nev. 202
Tonopah, Nev. 159
Town & Country 13, 46, 50
Trains in Transition 17, 62, 69, **218**
Treasure Island, San Francisco 15
Tremont & Gulf **105, 108**
Tunnel 1, Colo. 81, 83
Tweetsie, see: East Tennessee & Western North Carolina
Twentieth Century Limited [book] 207, 215
Twentieth Century Limited [train] 46, 205
Two Trains to Remember 207

U
Uintah Railway 156, 178
Unadilla Valley 49, **126**
Union Pacific 4, 42, **84, 85**, 87, **94**, 142, 178, 180, 181, 208
Union Pacific [film] 41, 42

V
Vinegar Bend, Ala. 112
Virginia City, Nev. 9, **11**, 18, **19**, 20, 21, 23, 28, **29**, 43, 192, 198, 205, 207, 208, 215, **224**
Virginia City (railroad car) 9, **21**, 22
Virginia & Truckee 9, 18, 28, 159, **192, 193, 194, 195, 196, 197, 198, 199, 200**, 207, 215

Virginia & Truckee: A Story of Virginia City and Comstock Times 19, 195, 199, 205

W
Wadley, Ga. **106**, 107
Wadley Southern 48, 104, **106, 107**
Wadsworth, Henry 100
Wakefield, Mass. 26, 36, 40
Walker, Stanley 38
Wallace, Hazzie 20, 21
Walsh, Clara Bell 15
Washington, D.C. 11, 13, 14, 15, 38
Washington Post 98
Washoe Canyon, Nev. **197**
Watertown, Mass. 55, 56
Watkins, Clarence 21
Weatherford, Mineral Wells & Northwestern **111**
West, Lavon see: Dimitri, Ivan
Western Pacific 17, 27, **52, 53**, 103, 153
When Beauty Rode the Rails 207, 208
Whitaker, Rogers E. M. (E. M. Frimbo) 55, 57
Whitman, Frederic B. 53
Wichita Falls & Southern **140**
Winchell, Walter 39, 55, 57
Winnfield, Louisiana 100, 105
Wright, Frank Lloyd 11
Wrightsville & Tennille **99**, 107
Wurm, Ted 198

Y
Yale University 38
Yee, Charlie 21
Yosemite Valley **146**
Youngstown, Ohio 14

Z
Zerbe, Jerome 14, 15, 33, 39, 42, 50

On the following two pages, a pile of rotting ties marks the end of San Luis Valley Southern tracks at Jaroso, Colorado. Beyond, only a herd of sheep occupy the lonely landscape. This is Clegg at his best in taking pictorial-style views. He seems to have included utility poles whenever possible in his pictures, perhaps because of his U.S. Navy service where ships' mastheads or scope lines defined scale, perspective, and linearity (*Mixed Train Daily*, page 349, *Great Railroad Photographs U.S.A.*, page 116). California State Railroad Museum, BC1404

Acknowledgments

The seed for this book was planted in 1953 in front of the *Territorial Enterprise* office in Virginia City, Nevada, when Lucius Beebe signed my copy of *Mixed Train Daily*.

Interest in Beebe and Charles Clegg expanded. Ann Clegg Holloway, sister of Charles, and Andria Daley, who then lived in the Beebe-Clegg home in Virginia City, contributed an article to *Vintage Rails* magazine ("Authors Celebrate Glory of Steam Era," No. 9, Fall 1997). The Holloways, including Ann's husband John Ennis when he was living, and Ann and Jack's children, Sally and Peter, have continued as supporters and their contributions have been a source of inspiration. They provided access to personal photographs of Beebe and Clegg; Daley added her extensive knowledge of Clegg and Beebe's activities in Virginia City and across the nation.

Reevaluation of their work began with a publication of Center for Railroad Photography & Art, *Railroad Heritage* no. 18, 2007, "Lucius Beebe and Charles Clegg, Railroading Journeys," which received an award from the Railway & Locomotive Historical Society.

At the California State Railroad Museum, where Ann and Jack Holloway placed the Beebe/Clegg collection, Paul Hammond, Cara Randall, and Ellen Halteman helped get this book off to a good start. Their successors, Ty Smith and Chris Rockwell, were enthusiastic and supported the completion of the book and the exhibition following its publication. Lisa Borok assisted in the library.

The Richard C. Overton Research Fellowship of the Lexington Group in Transportation History provided travel funds in 2016 and 2018, which assisted in research and allowed publication of preliminary articles in *Railroad History* and *Classic Trains*.

John Ryan and Mel Patrick joined in 2016, assisting with scanning and editing. Their hard work and insights made the book possible.

Frank Rapp and Michael McCreary, California residents, shared invaluable stories and information. Rapp and Clegg were friends; McCreary knew both Beebe and Clegg.

Gordon Crowell and Jim Ehernberger provided remembrances of meetings with Beebe and Clegg and examples of their own photographs published in Beebe-Clegg books. John W. "Jack" Barriger IV told about his family's travels with Beebe, Clegg, and Alfred and Adele Perlman on the narrow-gauge lines in Colorado and New Mexico.

Jack Holzhueter, Helen Ryan, and Ron Cady contributed editing skills.

Many people helped to identify photo locations, always a difficult task, and in other ways. They included James Bel-

John Gruber, Mel Patrick, and John Ryan in front of the Piper House in Virginia City, Nevada, in 2015. Patrick is wearing a top hat that once belonged to Lucius Beebe. Photo by Andria Daley

mont, Ted Benson, John Boehner, Kevin Bunker, Ray Buhrmaster, Charles Castner, Rich Gruber, Peyton Gupton, Bill Howes, Diane Laska-Swanke, Bennett Levin, Mel McFarland, Joe McMillan, Rich Millard, Wayne Monger, Steve Patterson, Angela Pusztai-Pasternak, Louis Saillard, Bill Schafer, Jamie Schmid, Josh Scott, Brian Solomon, Mike Del Vecchio, Jim Wrinn, and Tim Zukas. Thanks to these people, and others, captions in this book have more details than in many Beebe-Clegg books.

Phil Hamilton designed the dust jacket and assisted with design of the book.

The Center for Railroad Photography & Art provided the opportunity for a presentation at its 2016 conference. Scott Lothes and the Center's staff helped expedite the printing of this book. Thank you.

—John Gruber, March 2018